REIMAGINING THE GREAT COMMISSION

THE INTENTIONAL PRACTICE OF DISCIPLE MAKING

MARK BANE

THE FOUNDRY
PUBLISHING®

The Foundry Publishing®
PO Box 419527
Kansas City, MO 64141
thefoundrypublishing.com

978-0-8341-4341-8

Printed in the
United States of America

Cover design: Caines Design
Interior design: Sharon Page

Library of Congress Cataloging-in-Publication Data
A complete catalog record for this book is available from the Library of Congress.

The internet addresses, email addresses, and phone numbers in this book are accurate at the time of publication. They are provided as a resource. The Foundry Publishing does not endorse them or vouch for their content or permanence.

10 9 8 7 6 5 4 3 2 1

CONTENTS

PREFACE

The purpose of this book is to encourage, assist, equip, and engage Christians who have not been involved in disciple making personally. As I have traveled throughout the U.S. and Canada and all points in between over the past ten years, I've met many believers who *want* to be disciple makers. The problem is—and keep in mind this is my observation and is entirely anecdotal—more than 90 percent of the Christians I meet have never personally brought someone to faith.

I confess that I too am a reluctant evangelist. I have had thousands of encounters with pre-Christians, attempting to love them into the kingdom. Most have rejected the invitation. My success rate in bringing people to Jesus is not high. My best guess is that fewer than 10 percent of the individuals I've presented the gospel to have responded positively. That means 90 percent or more have said no.

My reluctance to share my faith is a result of my discomfort with rejection. I have yet to meet a person who enjoys rejection. Most believers I've met don't attempt evangelism at all because of similar fears. Aren't we grateful Jesus, Paul, and other New Testament leaders didn't retreat from the Great Commission for fear of rejection? Their example should be adequate inspiration to stimulate us to do the same.

A 2020 graph developed by the Jesus Film Project shows that fear is the number-one reason preventing believers from sharing their faith, according to the 1,600 Christians asked.

What prevents you from sharing your faith?

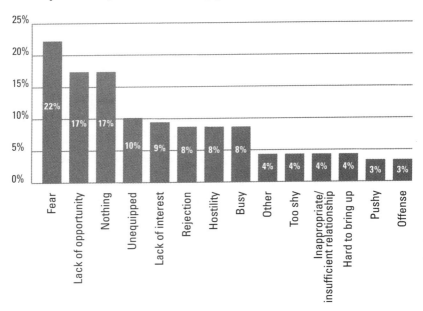

The goal of this book is to help those who have deep fears and other real reservations about evangelism and disciple making to overcome them and become what Jesus commissioned all believers to be: disciple makers. If you are one of the many Christians who have never personally embraced the Great Commission or if you have sat on the sidelines cheering on those who were engaged in disciple making but never personally invested in it yourself, this book is for you. I hope your commitment to and practice of disciple making will change by the time we are finished with this journey. We need you!

You are on the Jesus team, and there are no bleachers to fill. If you are a Christian, you are needed *in the game*. After forty years of pastoral ministry, one thing has become painfully apparent. Most believers are convinced they are doing their part if they are attending church, paying tithes, teaching a class, playing an instrument, singing or playing with the music team, participating in short-term mission trips, providing food at potlucks, and more. And of course, those activities are needed for the church to function effectively. However, none of those activities is the Great Commission. The Great Commission is to go and make disciples. If we are not making disciples, we must make a shift.

Scripture makes clear how important each of us is to the kingdom of God. Jesus reminded us in Matthew that "the harvest is plentiful but the workers are few" (9:37). The world of lost and broken people needs us to engage in disciple making. Jesus's vision was that the world would be saved through him. It is not his will that any perish but that all come to repentance. I pray you will seek God and ask the question, "Do you want me to be a disciple maker?" I think we know what God's answer will be!

INTRODUCTION

In order to reimagine the Great Commission, we first have to reimagine our understanding of the church. Whom is the Great Commission directed to? Is Jesus commissioning an organization to go make disciples, or is he commissioning individuals?

The church doesn't *have* a mission. The church *is* the mission—or, better: the mission has a church. The church is God's plan to win the world. By "the church," I don't mean the building down the street where people gather to sing, read Scripture together, listen to sermons, pray, and have potlucks. That is *a* church—a local church. By "the church," I mean the people of God—many of whom can be found in that building down the street—who are on mission. The church is *you*—if you have come to trust Jesus as your Savior and Lord. You, me—we are *the* church.

As the title suggests, this is not a book on evangelism theology. You can find all sorts of books in Christian libraries with titles like *The Theology of Evangelism, Evangelical Theology,* or *A Theological Mandate.* Those books have a different purpose than this one. This book focuses on the practice of *disciple making,* which is the most underserved element of evangelism in contemporary church culture.

We could get into all kinds of theological dart-throwing and semantic exchanges that might further promote a particular preference or expertise related to evangelism, but that is not the goal of this book. Rather, this book aims to assist believers in the one practice Jesus commanded and commissioned us all to do: go and make disciples of all nations!

Unfortunately, most Christians have spent their entire Christian lives learning the disciplines of the faith, developing prayer habits, reading and learning the Bible, practicing corporate worship, and developing stewardship practices—while ignoring or avoiding Jesus's command to go make disciples of all the nations. We seek to answer two questions here:

1) Is it possible for every Christian to be a disciple maker?
2) How can Christians move from being disciples to being disciple makers?

As we begin this journey together, consider some of the following perspectives and truths.

1. There is no such thing as an average Christian.

No Christian is average, in the sense of "mediocre" or "unimpressive." There are all sorts of Christians. There are quiet ones who want to live their lives without the bother of the troubles in the world around them. They may be quiet, but if they are Christian, they are not average. There are introverted Christians who wish to disengage from the stress of multiple new relationships. They may be introverted, but they are not average.

A Christian possesses the Spirit of God. This possession makes us larger than the sum of our parts.

It gives us the Spirit of Jesus, the Spirit of power, love, and self-control (see 2 Timothy 1:7).

It gives us the gift of a faith that can move mountains—and not by taking ten thousand people, ten thousand shovels, and ten thousand pickup trucks more than ten thousand years to move a mountain.

The mountain-moving faith of a Christian can only be explained by the miraculous hand of God (see Matthew 17:20; 21:21).

It causes us to do all the same sorts of things Jesus did—and even greater things (see John 14:12).

It gives the power to heal the sick, to love those who hate us, to be good to those who persecute us and say all manner of evil against us falsely. It teaches us to say no to ungodliness and worldly passions, to live upright and godly lives in this present age while we wait for the blessed hope—the appearing of the glory of our great God and Savior, Jesus Christ.

It gives us everything we need for a godly life. It causes us to participate in the divine nature and escape the corruption in the world caused by evil desires. And it causes us to live a life exceedingly abundantly above all we could ever ask or imagine!

Does that sound average to you? I am convinced by both Scripture and sound reason that no Christian is average. Christians are the chosen, blessed, gifted, empowered, and equipped people of God! Nothing is average about that.

2. Every believer can and should be a disciple maker.

I say this emphatically because I believe there is no such thing as an average Christian. Regardless of one's personality, gifting, skills, training, background, upbringing, or anything else, every believer is empowered to make disciples. It is not our natural human abilities that empower us but our God-given nature upon becoming a Christian. Disciple making is more about will than skill. Disciple making is more about the power of God than one's personal attributes. Not every believer will make disciples in the same way or at the same rate, but every believer should be a disciple maker by the command of Jesus. Disciple making is not reserved for the extroverted, the gifted evangelist, the well-trained, or the experienced practitioner—it is for every believer in Christ.

3. Disciple making is not a duty to be performed, an obligation to fulfill, or a burden to lift. It is a thrill to experience!

Disciple making is the crescendo of our faith! It is the highest and most cathartic experience believers will ever have. I have heard the "old-timers" talk about how the glory fell in the old camp meetings and revival services. I was there for some of them, and enjoyed them immensely. I received the Holy Spirit at one of those events. I remember the thrill of seeing people humble themselves before God. These are awesome experiences for which I will be forever grateful.

However, these experiences pale in comparison to the joy and exhilaration that come when a believer leads someone to authentic faith in Jesus. It is better than watching the metamorphosis of a caterpillar to a butterfly. As amazing as that is, of course, it is a natural occurrence. Seeing a transformed life is *supernatural* and cannot be adequately described. Watching such a transformation is amazing, but experiencing it as a disciple maker is extraordinary!

4. I wish, dream about, pray for, and long for the day that every believer on Planet Earth experiences the exhilaration of bringing someone to Jesus (or bringing Jesus to someone) and watching the transformation firsthand.

We first have to believe it is possible for every believer. If we think it is exhilarating for us, imagine heaven's reaction! Jesus said, "I tell you that in the same way there will be more rejoicing in heaven over one sinner who repents than over ninety-nine righteous persons who do not need to repent" (Luke 15:7). My prayer for this book is that it advances that goal.

5. There are some church leaders who proclaim that disciple making is only for those who are gifted in that unique way and that not everyone is, but if you are a Christian, your part is to make disciples—nothing less.

The Word of God says that all Christians are called to help fulfill the Great Commission by making disciples—regardless of status, expertise, gifting, or personality. The Father has commissioned us, equipped us, and sent us out to make disciples. Our response must be: *Yes, Lord, yes! I will obey as you provide the direction, tools, and opportunities.* Jesus said, "In the same way your Father in heaven is not willing that any of these little ones should perish" (Matthew 18:14). The only possible way for the entire world to come to faith is if every believer is engaged in disciple making.

To discourage any Christian from pursuing the Great Commission because of personality, lack of courage, fear, lack of training, or any other reason would be to stand against the very God who calls us to go make disciples.

I experienced this temptation in my early Christian life by becoming so overwhelmed with the call to lead the church that I came to God with prayers of desperation: "God I am so busy leading a youth group, I really don't have time to make disciples personally."

God's response? *Your first responsibility as a Christian is to make disciples; if there is any time left, you can be a youth pastor.*

The overwhelming responsibility of pastoring an entire church was the next call and responsibility I received. I will never forget coming to God in frustration and desperation: "Father, I am so overwhelmed with the responsibilities of being a good father, a good husband, a prayer warrior, organizing the church schedule, developing leaders, planning events, going to seminars, and more—I don't have time to be involved in personal disciple making."

Again, the Lord made it clear: *Mark, your first responsibility as a believer is to be a disciple maker. Do that first, and there will be ample time, resource, and energy to do the other things I have called you to do.* (See Matthew 6:33.)

Next, becoming a district superintendent added a new sense of responsibility and a lifestyle that made disciple making feel almost impossible because of all my travel. I felt like Paul: "Besides everything else, I face daily the pressure of my concern for all the churches" (2 Corinthians 11:28.)

Yet the answer from the Lord did not change: *Mark, your first responsibility as a Christian is to be a disciple maker. If you do this, I will make sure you have the time, resource, and energy to do the other things as well. Seek me first, and the other things will be added to you.*

My Personal Journey with Disciple Making

Disciple making is stewardship of resources. If we put what really matters to God first, he will make sure the other things are cared for better than we could if we put them first. I am convinced that when things are in this order, our lives are balanced and we are most fulfilled; we become the best spouses, the best parents, the best pastors, the best church leaders in any capacity—when we put what matters most to the Master first. The Great Commission is what matters. The Spirit has to remind me daily: *the Great Commission is not a suggestion.*

Are you actively making disciples? If not, this book can help!

In 1976, I was a new, excited believer. Uninformed in all things Christian, I had just been delivered from a life of drugs, alcohol, tobacco, sexual sin, lawlessness, and violence. It is hard to imagine all of that at only age seventeen, but it is true. I was a good sinner who moved through the ranks of sindom at a rapid pace. I excelled at messing up my life. I had almost become an expert at disobeying God and pursuing my own agenda. I found it didn't take long for Satan to really ruin a young life.

What I didn't realize until later was that I was born into a fallen world where sin reigned, contrary to God's original intent. We all were! Although we were all created in the image of God, the power of the sinful nature is very strong! After a brief encounter with a Jesus freak one month shy of my eighteenth birthday (more details later about that experience and my regeneration and conversion as a Christian), Jesus changed my life.

Following this radical transformation, I quickly found a church (after much research and investigation) and began making Christian friends and leaving my old life. Even my old friends were left behind in the dust of my exciting new ride. In retrospect, that part was a mistake. Somehow in the newness, naïveté, and excitement of the church experience, my new Christian friends failed to mention something essential. My first Christian move should not have been to leave old friends in the dust of my past life. I should have walked with them through the dust and brought them along with me. I will regret for the rest of my days the pain that could have been avoided in the lives of my old friends, had I been given better guidance in the early days of my faith. I am sure Jesus tried to encourage me to attempt to reach my old friends who were so lost. I am not sure I even knew how to listen to God in those early days. This is a problem for so many people of faith. We spend more time talking than listening to the Master in our prayers. I have a sense that, if we really focused on listening more carefully to Jesus, we might hear similar admonitions to the one he gave the healed demoniac in the Gerasenes: "The man from whom the demons had gone out begged to go with him, but Jesus sent him away, saying, 'Return home and tell how much God has done for you.' So the man went away and told all over town how much Jesus had done for him" (Luke 8:38–39).

This failure is not just mine, however; it is one of the great failures of the contemporary church. When someone comes to faith, we often postpone passing on the imperative to go make disciples. Instead, we wait until they are more mature or better prepared. We should do as Jesus modeled in both the story of the Samaritan woman in John 4 and the healing of the demoniac in Luke 8. The first thing a new believer should be counseled to do is tell others what Jesus has done for them. The first action, in light of Jesus's words "Come, follow me . . . and I will send you out to fish for people" (Matthew 4:19) should be to send them back to fish for pre-Christians. New Christians should become an instant bridge to their pre-Christian friends. I was so caught up in the pursuit of holiness, righteousness, and good churchmanship that I missed the single most central mission of every believer, regardless of years of service or maturity level of their faith: *be a disciple maker.*

It took me a while to understand the truth that it is not an either-or proposition (i.e., either grow in life/parenting/marriage relationship/faith/purity, *or* grow in discipling). It is both a grow-*and*-make-disciples proposition.

Thanks be to God, unlike most new believers, I was rescued by a Christian friend who helped me break out of self-righteous patterns that hinder so many young Christians whose lives are driven by duty, obligation, and ritual rather than the freedom that comes from putting God and his wishes ahead of our own. Just a few weeks into my new faith journey, as I strove to fit into a new social construct the church was framing for me, I had what I later learned was a rare encounter. I ran into someone who took the Great Commission very seriously.

One evening after Sunday night service at my local church, a Christian friend asked me, "Are you now a Christian?"

I responded passionately, "Absolutely!"

He said, "Okay, then you need to go witnessing."

I thought, *I'm being called to jury duty this soon after leaving my previous life of crime?* In those early days, biblical literacy was a real deficiency for me. I wondered what crime I was going to be a witness for. I was on the wrong train of thought on that "witnessing" stuff.

My friend said, "Now that you are a Christian, you need to tell others about what happened to you. That is what witnessing is. Meet me Friday evening at Shoney's, and I will show you what I mean."

I was young and pliable, so I showed up to the Shoney's parking lot with fear and uncertainty. After a few instructions, we went in to do that "witness" thing.

His instructions were simple:

1. Sit down to order a coffee, and begin praying that God sends someone who needs Jesus to sit next to you.

2. Take this little booklet. It was a religious tract that told the story of a man who lived a wicked life then died and faced judgment, landing in hell. At the end of the pamphlet was a prayer to help the reader learn how to avoid such a terrible fate.

3. Do nothing but wait until someone sits down. When someone does, say to them, "God loves you, and I love you, and God has an amazing plan for your life."

4. Then hand them the tract and say, "This little booklet will help you understand better what I am saying."

5. Then say, "God bless you," and pause to see if they have any questions.

6. If they have no questions, leave them alone, return to your coffee, and begin praying for that person, asking God to help them be responsive to the encounter and to the booklet you left with them.

Okay, I thought, *I can do this.*

So we entered Shoney's, sat down at the bar (not the kind that serves alcohol but the old diner kind that allowed strangers to sit close to one another and interact if they wished, which they often did), and ordered coffee (the new Christian 'drug'). It was my first cup of coffee ever, and it was awful. However, I wanted to fit in, so I put so much cream and sugar in it that it was almost tolerable. While I didn't like coffee, I did learn to like the "coffee pudding" made from the cream and sugar. That has never changed. I now love some "coffee pudding."

After about ten minutes, a very large man entered the restaurant. I noticed he had driven up in a tractor trailer. He was a beast of a man, resembling Sasquatch. It has been a long time, some forty-seven years, so my memory is not clear about all the details, but I do clearly remember he was a big dude. And he was scary.

My prayers instantly shifted to my safety: "Lord, please don't let him sit next to me!" I hadn't learned yet to be careful what I pray for. He sat right next to me.

As I sat there wordlessly, my friend stuck his elbow into my ribs from the other side, encouraging me to go do the witnessing thing he had prepared me for. After about three of these nudges, I looked at him and said, "I will witness to him if and when the Holy Spirit tells me to. Thank you very much!"

He said, "The Holy Spirit told you to do this two thousand years ago in the Great Commission. Stop stalling and making excuses. Go do what the Bible said."

Well, he knew the Bible better than I did, so I began. I approached this stranger with these opening words: "Hi, my name is Mark, and I want to share some really great news with you today. God loves you, I love you, and God has an amazing plan for your life." And I held out the booklet.

With a low growl in his voice, he answered, "I don't talk religion, and I don't read about religion, so take this booklet, get out of here, and stop bothering me!"

He then threw the tract and hit me in the chest with it. After picking it up from the counter, I quickly scurried off and began praying.

Fortunately, he left just after that. I watched in great relief as he drove his tractor trailer out of the parking. He had been pretty violent, so I was happy it was over.

I had lived through my first witnessing experience. Whew! His immediate response might make anyone want to quit and never witness again. That was my thinking at the moment.

After praying for about fifteen minutes and having a direct discussion with my friend (whom I viewed as the source of this bad experience), I noticed Sasquatch and his rig pulling back into the restaurant parking lot. That was not a good sign. I knew he was going to escalate his violent behavior.

All I knew to do was to pray harder, and maybe he would leave me alone, so I put my hands together in front of my face to give a clear message. It didn't deter him in the least. He walked right up to me. I could feel him standing just beside me.

Not looking up, I continued to pray, now with my hands more definitively posed. You could have made a sculpture of praying hands out of my posture! The message was clear: *Don't interrupt me. I'm talking to God.*

He didn't care. The urgency of his wishes trumped my prayer facade.

I felt a heavy finger on my right shoulder. I thought, *Now it is on!*

I didn't know what to do in that moment. Before I became a Christian, it would have been easy. Just be ready to fight back. But now I had heard about this "turn the other cheek" stuff. To be honest, that philosophy I had not yet fully assimilated into my life.

I looked up, and, to my utter shock, he looked deeply into my eyes with large tears flowing down his cheeks. He said, "Young man, I am sorry for my behavior earlier. Would you please put this in the plate for me on Sunday?" He handed me several wadded-up dollar bills and walked off with his head hanging down.

I was amazed. The question ran through my mind: *Did God speak to him as he drove off that day? How could someone so mean and violent change so fast?*

That was my first experience witnessing to a stranger. I am so glad God led my friend to force me into that experience. I learned so much about disciple making. Although no disciple was made that I could see, I had survived the experience and I did get to see God work on a human being to soften a heart. I have never forgotten it.

What strikes me today is how few believers ever get the privilege of being put in a situation to see how God can work. I wish every believer could have such an experience early in their faith journey. I had the blessing of a coach to help me through the challenges of the discouragement that comes from rejection while celebrating how God can work when we take risks. Otherwise, fear and insecurity could have won the day and stopped me from ever witnessing again.

Because so few North American Christians today are engaged in evangelism, I'm guessing you don't have the advantage of an experience like mine. Few are modeling it, and as a result, few are doing it. I pray this will change. My experience at Shoney's that day gave me an edge in the disciple-making process, blessing me with the privilege, early in my faith, of seeing God's Spirit work, even through awkward and uncomfortable circumstances. I learned that initiating a conversation with a stranger, even if done poorly, can end well. My own salvation story, which I will share in chapter 2, is another example of this same thing.

To be clear, my Shoney's experience is not the best model of an evangelism effort. I was way too young in my faith to have a mature understanding of evangelism and disciple making. Yet I do believe that personal evangelism, the style I was taught to use that day, can be an effective method of sharing the gospel. Yet time and experience have taught us that establishing a connection with someone that leads to authentic relationship is generally *more* effective in the effort to bring persons to faith than a cold contact with little or no relational history.

We should always seek to establish relationships when we share the gospel, rather than practicing a hit-and-run approach. However, we also should never resist sharing our faith with a stranger when we are led by the Spirit to do so. There are many examples in Scripture of lives being changed through chance encounters with little relational history or engagement. Consider Jonah and the

Ninevites, Jesus and Zacchaeus, the Samaritan woman at the well, Philip and the Ethiopian eunuch, and Jesus with the criminal hanging beside him on the cross. These stories show us that God can use all kinds of situations and scenarios to bring someone to faith and bear great fruit. The Great Commission is not an instruction simply to evangelize but to *make disciples.*

The pressing question must always be: *are pre-Christians coming to faith through our lives?* That is the question the Great Commission begs us to answer. We must guard against arguments, criticisms, and attempts to deconstruct forms of evangelism we may not personally appreciate. There are many forms of evangelism that will bear fruit and bring people to Jesus when done well. When we focus on the question, "Are people coming to faith through my life?" then we can reevaluate our personal disciple-making activity and methods if the answer is no.

D. L. Moody made this point well in a memorable encounter with a woman who criticized the methods of evangelism he employed in his attempt to win people to Jesus. He said, "I don't like the way I do it either. Tell me, how do you do it?"

The woman replied, "I don't do it."

His reply was, "I like my way of doing it better than your way of not doing it."

These three points of advice will go a long way for those seeking to fulfill the Great Commission:

- **Find a form of evangelism and disciple making that works for you and practice that one**. If you can't find one you feel comfortable with, ask God for help. God is so creative and can guide you into ways of bringing people to Jesus that maybe no one has ever practiced before.

- **Any form of disciple making should be continually examined for its ongoing effectiveness in our changing world and across various cultures.** I have been in the church long enough to observe those who practice personal evangelism criticizing those who practice relational evangelism, and those who practice relational evangelism criticizing those who practice attractional evangelism. Criticism for criticism's sake is not productive for building up the body of Christ or fulfilling the Great Commission. Yet the world is continually changing, so we ought to remain open to methodical tweaks and enhancements designed to improve the overall outcome of our common goal. May we all embrace the apostle Paul's perspective: "I have become all things to all people so that by all possible means I might save some" (1 Corinthians 9:22).

- **Beware of the temptation to judge disciple-making methods as effective or ineffective based on visible or immediate results.** Scholars have suggested that even Jesus did not see the full fruit of his ministry until after his resurrection. Stephen certainly didn't see the full fruit of his first and only sermon, since he was stoned to death immediately afterward. He didn't live to see that his death for the sake of the gospel was probably the catalyst that led to the greatest evangelist of the New Testament, Saul/Paul, coming to faith in Christ. God keeps working long after we stop.

After I had several more experiences like my first Shoney's encounter, sharing my faith became second nature. Experiencing rejection became part of the framework I grew to expect as normative. I am still active in disciple making. Because of my intentional evangelistic activity, some assume and proclaim that I have the gift of evangelism, which I suppose is possible. The more likely explanation, however, is that I've been blessed with lots of experience in doing evangelism—not always because of my own volition. At first, I really didn't think my initial experience was a great one. I never would have ventured out to Shoney's on my own that evening. My friend was pushy. He practiced a definition of leadership I am learning to embrace: the art of annoying people at a rate they can tolerate. I am eternally grateful for that night and the many like it that followed.

The Purpose of Spiritual Gifts

It is true that some have been specifically given the gift of evangelism. However, according to Paul in Ephesians 4:11–14, the primary reason for giving those gifts was not so that those who had the gift would be the only ones practicing them. Rather, the gifts were to be used to equip the body of believers with those gifts so that the whole body of Christ performs works of service until we all reach the fullness of Christ. In other words, we were given the gifts so that we could gift them to the body. Maybe I only have the gift of evangelism because my friend passed his gift on to me. Maybe this is what Paul had in mind for the church.

We tend to disqualify ourselves from evangelism if we are not naturals at it. I don't know if anyone is a natural at evangelism. I am more convinced every day that it is more like other activities we *become* good at. Take a doctor, for example. Most doctors would not say they are naturally gifted at doctoring—I have asked many! The answer overwhelmingly is, "I am good at it because I spent nine to ten years studying and practicing medicine, and several more years as an intern. Finally, after all that, I had the confidence to help people improve their health."

I have asked many physicians, "Was it scary the first time you were in a room alone with a patient? Were you afraid you might mess up the diagnosis or miss something?"

The answer is always a resounding yes!

What if the Great Commission is not just for the few exceptionally gifted? What if God's plan to win his world is that every believer goes through the fire of practicing evangelism, making mistakes occasionally and being imperfect until confidence is built? Each believer then becomes capable of participating in the work of the Great Commission, even if we don't all have the specific spiritual gift of evangelism. Maybe getting the gift means receiving it from someone like my friend until we become proficient at it—then, BOOM, we have the gift.

Is This Book for You?

According to Scripture, every believer is called to do Great Commission work, but not all are gifted by the Spirit to practice it with ease. That is why I wrote this book. If you've been wondering whether this book is for you, consider these questions:

- Have you wanted to be a disciple maker but never worked up the courage? *This book is for you.*
- Have you attempted to do evangelism and only experienced rejection? *This book is for you.*
- Are you an introvert who has lived your Christian life believing the secular myth that disciple making is only for extroverts? *This book is for you.*

- Have you gone on one of those Saturday morning door-knocking adventures with your church only to have doors slammed in your face? *This book is for you.*
- Have you had the experience of encountering a gifted evangelist only to go away thinking you could never be like that because you don't have the same skills and gifts? *This book is for you.*
- Are you a mature Christian, maybe even in leadership in the church, yet you know the one thing you've neglected is making a disciple, and you are afraid to confess it out loud? *This book is for you!*

The purpose of this book is to encourage, inspire, assist, equip, and engage Christians who have not been involved in disciple making or who have had bad experiences with disciple making. The ultimate goal is to assist every believer to become involved in disciple making again or for the first time.

A Disciple-Making Crisis

While traveling throughout the U.S. and Canada over the past ten years, I've met thousands of good Christians who would love to make a disciple. The problem is that 95 percent of them have never personally discipled anyone to faith.

One of hundreds of these observations took place at a large event with six or seven hundred pastors, leaders, and laity from sixty-two churches of all sizes. I posed the question: "How many of you here have served God for at least thirty years?"

About 95 percent stood in response. It was a graying group.

Then I said, "Please remain standing if you can identify someone who has come to Christ through your personal discipleship activities. If not, please be seated."

Everyone sat down, except about eight people. So, less than 2 percent of that group of church leaders and pastors confessed to ever having made a new disciple! I was staggered, and assumed it was the exception to the rule. However, I have continued to ask these questions in presentations to similar groups over the past ten years, and the numbers don't change much. Less than 5 percent of the multiple thousands of pastors, leaders, and laity I have asked this question of in the past ten years have been personally involved with disciple making of any kind.

These observations are somewhat anecdotal, but personal experience tells me the numbers are similar all over North America. If the Great Commission is to make disciples, we are failing at a rate that is almost unimaginable. The declining church attendance numbers affirm this to be true. The church in North America is on the verge of many crises:

1. **Attendance**: According to a 2024 Gallup poll, only 30 percent of U.S. adults regularly attend religious services. This is a sharp decline from 42 percent in 2000.

2. **Finances**: Many churches have had to transition their pastors from full-time vocational ministry to part-time, bi-vocational, or co-vocational ministry, leading to the next problem—fewer being willing to serve.

3. **Leader Shortages**: According to the 2020 Faith Communities Today (FACT) study, the average age of religious leaders in the United States was fifty-seven years old, up from fifty in 2000. The NCS also reports that the median age of lead

pastors increased from forty-nine to fifty-seven years old between 1998 and 2019.

If every believer in every church took disciple making seriously, we would not be having these crises. If every Christian took disciple making seriously, we would have more people, more leaders, more dollars, than we would know what to do with. Jesus had a great idea—the Great Commission! A disciple-making shortage is the biggest crisis the church faces. As other aspects of the church decline, the pool of believers who take disciple making seriously is also declining. Pre-Christians now have fewer opportunities to hear about the amazing life of faith.

Nobody likes rejection. Jesus didn't, Paul didn't, and neither do we. Yet it is clear in Scripture how important each of us is to the kingdom. The world needs us all to engage in disciple making. Jesus's vision was that the *world* would be saved through him. It is not his will that any perish but that *all* come to repentance!

I pray you will seek God and pray daily, "Do you want me to be a disciple maker?" I think you know what the answer will be.

Everyone who wants to examine their disciple-making intentions and activities seriously should ask themselves the following questions:

1. Are new believers coming to faith through my life and ministry?

2. If not, why not?

3. What can I do to change that?

Let's plunge into these and other questions that beg for an answer.

Questions for New Disciple Makers

1. Have you ever attempted to share your faith with a stranger?

2. If yes, what was the response?

3. If you thought it would make a meaningful difference in someone's life, would you be willing to risk rejection?

4. What are your greatest reservations, objections, or fears about sharing your faith with a stranger?

5. Where in your daily life might you have opportunities to begin relationships with those who may not yet have faith in Jesus?

6. Would you be willing to commit to praying the following four prayers every morning?

   A. *Father, help me to have a broken heart for the same things that break your heart.*

   B. *Lord, please guide me to the people you want me to impact today.*

   C. *Please give me the courage to initiate conversations when it is your will.*

   D. *Help me be prepared to share my faith when your Spirit calls me to do so.*

ONE

THE DIFFERENCE BETWEEN EVANGELISM AND DISCIPLE MAKING

This chapter is designed to illuminate the difference between the Great Commission ("go and make disciples") and the evangelistic work of sharing or presenting the gospel. Both are essential to fulfilling the mission of Jesus. Disciple making is a long-term investment in someone's life, beyond a one-time encounter. There will be occasions, if we are daily on mission, when we share our faith with someone we may never see again. Praise God for these times when the Spirit uses us to give good news to a stranger. This was my story of coming to faith. However, with the exception of these rare occasions, making a disciple usually takes much time and much investment.

We want to drill down into personal disciple-making follow-up here. My experience tells me poor follow-up is the primary reason for ineffective disciple making. Lack of effective follow-up is the main reason most evangelistic attempts fail to lead to making Christlike disciples. If our goal is to help believers make disciples rather than just do evangelism, follow-up becomes essential. Disciples will not be made with only a one-hour-a-week-on-Sunday investment. Disciple making means long-term relational investment and sacrifice in and for another human being. We should go into evangelism with our eyes wide open. The singular reason most Christians are not making disciples today is that it is hard work that includes passionate prayer, intentional meetings, and life-on-life engagement.

To illustrate the investment necessary, I will share two stories. The first is personal. After moving to Gainesville, Florida, three years ago, I sensed God's call to plant a church in the urban core. I knew it would be challenging because my work schedule had me traveling for some twenty to twenty-five days out of every month. However, knowing God will never call us to do anything we can't accomplish with his help, the planting journey began. The first task in starting the church was to find a first person of peace—that first person who could become our first Christian, and possible first leader.

My morning routine usually gets started around three thirty and four o'clock a.m., off to McDonald's for a morning coffee, then to the office by four thirty and five a.m. Because disciple making is so important, my morning prayers always include these five requests:

1. Help me find people today who don't yet know you.

2. Help me engage the right people in conversation.

3. Give me the courage to initiate conversations when necessary.

4. Give me the wisdom to know what words to speak that could lead to life.

5. Give me the insight to find a way to reconnect with those I meet.

One particular morning in the spring of 2021 I was following my routine and getting my McDonald's coffee. Jackie was working that morning, and we had the first of several conversations over a three-week period, lasting only a few seconds.

On the morning of my sixth encounter with Jackie in the McDonald's drive-thru window, I had prayed my five prayers as usual, and this visit was different. I was there just as the store was opening, and there was no one behind me at the drive-thru, so we had a few rare minutes to chat.

After a brief greeting, I said, "I am headed to the office for prayer time. Is there anything I can pray for you about?"

I was amazed at how open she was to share intimate details of the challenges she was facing at home, particularly with her teenage son, who was creating weekly havoc, leading to extra expense for her—a single mom of six who works at McDonald's. As it turned out, there was trouble with the law, and she needed seven hundred dollars to get him out of the trouble.

I was honored that she was willing to share such details with a stranger. It told me she was really interested in prayer and probably God. Often when Christians encounter needy persons with money issues, especially in urban areas, they are immediate skeptical, which is sometimes warranted, but in this case, God cleared up the question for me later on.

Offering to pray for someone, and then actually doing it, can accelerate the deepening of a relationship. Every time the prayer question is asked, I am amazed how vulnerable and honest people can be. It is an incredible trust that can lead to a wonderful friendship. Praying for a stranger should be the first steps in disciple making!

After that encounter with Jackie, travel took me away for two weeks. During that time, I prayed for Jackie and her son daily. When I returned home, I couldn't wait to see her and help with her financial burden because my prayers had given me clear guidance to get involved in Jackie's life and attempt to help her. I decided that I could assist Jackie with a gift of four hundred dollars. The next morning at the drive-thru, I asked Jackie if she would be willing to meet with me outside of work to discuss how I could help. She was willing, and she brought her son to our meeting, where I offered her the cash.

To my amazement, she turned it down, saying, "Thank you, but I already took care of this need. We are good, but thanks for caring enough to offer."

The next time I met with her, a month later, I had a chance to meet her family. I called one afternoon and offered to bring dinner to her family, and she agreed. What I didn't know at the time was that her family situation consisted of about a dozen people sharing a two-bedroom apartment. But I had the chance that day to meet and spend an hour or so with twelve new friends who would eventually become part of the new church plant, thanks be to God.

Over the next year we shared many meals and had lots of chances to engage in many settings. Jackie and I had become friends. Her family was very interested in helping me start a church, so I began to invite them to our monthly Bible studies. At our first meeting there were seven. The next time, Jackie had invited so many people she needed help with transportation. With a new set of friends who seemed interested in Jesus, the possibilities looked great! Taking the time to invest in people, and showing authentic care and concern for their lives and troubles, opens the door for the gospel in a way that nothing else can.

While driving Jackie and her family members to Bible study that second night, I prayed, "Lord, please make tonight a good experience for Jackie and her family."

God seemed to say to me, as clear as could be, *"Ask her if she would like to become a Christian."*

I thought, *Isn't it a little soon, Father?*

No response from God. He wasn't interested in arguing. That meant he was serious.

At the next stoplight, I asked Jackie the question.

Her response was immediate: "Absolutely!"

Surprised and amazed, I went through a simple gospel presentation right there in the car, using John 3:16 as my text. She knew John 3:16 well enough to quote it to me. She had some church background in what she identified as a cult, but at least they got that verse correct.

John 3:16 can be used as a simple step-by-step way to help someone become a Christian:

1. The fact: God loves you more than you can imagine.
2. The act: God loves you so much that he showed his love by sending his Son to become human for the sake of saving all humanity.
3. The pact: Whoever believes in him will not perish but have eternal life.

As a disciple maker, it's important to learn a method of leading someone to Christ that is comfortable for you. If in doubt, consider googling a method or looking for a YouTube tutorial! People use YouTube for everything these days, from cooking a new recipe to fixing something they have never repaired before. Type into Google or YouTube "how to present the gospel of Jesus to someone" and you will find more answers than you can imagine. It is not a matter of skill but of will!

After asking a few questions, Jackie prayed and accepted Christ. That night at Bible study, we celebrated her new life in Christ.

Being hyper sensitive to the Holy Spirit, having the courage to do what the Spirit asks, and trusting God for the results are essential components of disciple making.

Jackie and her kids and I have become good friends. Whenever I am in Gainesville, we get together. The church plant still has Bible study monthly, and she and her family have never missed one. She is growing in faith and leadership, and Jackie was a strong influence in bringing her son Jun and daughter Kira to faith. She regularly witnesses to others in her apartment complex, and she assisted in organizing an outreach event where we were able to feed and love on 137 of her neighbors, which led to four new families getting connected with our church.

Disciple making will not be accomplished through only a one-hour-a-week investment in people. It doesn't take skill but will. Intentional follow-up is essential to disciple making.

The final illustration requires me to introduce two main characters who are from different worlds and will help us see the investment it can take to see someone move from where they are to where God wants them to be.

I have a very special ministry partner in my life named Jenee Noriega. Jenee was severely abused as a child, first molested at age five. She quit school in the seventh grade and took her first hit of crack-cocaine at age eleven. At age sixteen she made the Most Wanted list in New Mexico. She was arrested twenty-four times before age nineteen. She spent almost a decade locked up. She was a misguided, drug-addicted, needy young woman. Her first two children were conceived and born in addiction.

One of my faith heroes is another woman named Debbie Van Hook. Debbie is a multi-generational Christian who was raised in the church and has been faithfully serving God pretty much her entire life. She would be a stellar model of Christianity in any church that had the good pleasure of her ministry partnership.

Jenee and Debbie are two people who come from different backgrounds, lifestyles, and cultures, and God used Debbie to bring Jenee to Jesus. Debbie began investing in Jenee's life about twenty years ago. Jenee had become connected to Debbie's church through one of their many outreach ministries. They had a thrift store that served as an official Community Service Partner with the city corrections department, which meant that if someone wanted to avoid a short-term incarceration, they could choose to do hours of community service instead.

After one of her arrests, Jenee chose to do community service at the church's thrift store. As she worked folding flyers for one of the outreach events the church was planning, she asked someone about the event, and then attended the event herself. After visiting additional outreach events, and a church service or two, Jenee met Debbie, and they made an unlikely connection. Jenee and Debbie had nothing except Jesus in common—Debbie served him, and Jenee knew she needed him.

After a brief conversation, Jenee told Debbie, "Please just don't forget me!"

Leading up to her connection with Jenee, Debbie had been praying intensely that God would help her do a better job of making disciples of the pre-Christians her church's annual outreach events ministered to each year. They saw hundreds, sometimes thousands, of people make initial professions of faith, but without follow-up from mature disciples of Christ, many of the new Christians often fell away before they became disciples.

As a result of her prayers and her desire to be a disciple maker, Debbie decided to really invest in, care for, and love her new friend. The challenges to their relationship continued to grow when Jenee was arrested again and went to jail. After she bonded out the next day, she called Debbie on the way home from jail and asked Debbie to come and talk with her more about Jesus.

Debbie recalls, "I was scared to death to go over there alone." Debbie called her mentor, Rev. Jan Sweeney, and asked Jan to go with her.

Jan used great wisdom by telling Debbie, "She called you, Debbie. This is something you need to do."

So Debbie went that day prayerfully, with great fear and trepidation.

Yet, through Debbie's faithfulness to the Great Commission, Jenee was delivered that day from a nineteen-year drug addiction, and she started a new life of faith.

Debbie wanted Jenee's commitment to life in Christ to stick, so she began visiting regularly, picking up Jenee and her family for church, taking her to weeknight Bible studies, bringing food when needed, and praying daily for her development as a believer.

There were setbacks. Jenee fell off the wagon once and stole the pastor's car on a drug binge. She was incarcerated again for thirty days. Debbie organized care for Jenee's children during that time so that social services would not take them away. Debbie estimates that she often invested as many as ten hours a week in her relationship with Jenee, for years.

Debbie's faithfulness bore great fruit. Today, Jenee is serving God, pastoring a growing church, has completed undergraduate and master's degrees, and is working on a doctorate. She is a highly regarded public speaker throughout North America. Her husband, children, and many of her friends and relatives also serve Jesus today because of the investment of one woman who had never stepped out of her comfort zone before in pursuit of becoming a disciple maker.

The church that equipped Debbie to disciple Jenee employed all six forms of disciple making that we will discuss in chapter 6 in their efforts to, by all means, win some. Jenee was a stranger who was invited into church fellowship. She was a hungry person who was fed at outreach events. She was visited in prison by faithful church members. Jenee was introduced to Jesus through multiple people and multiple avenues, both individually and corporately, and the follow-up planted the seeds for Jenee to become a disciple maker herself.

Follow-up and life-on-life engagement are the best ways to make a solid disciple of Christ. Jenee says of Debbie and that faith community, "That church just wouldn't quit. They never gave up on me."

For her part, Debbie was willing to make several significant changes in her schedule, routine, and habits over five years' time in order to assist Jenee to become a disciple of Jesus. Often, the contemporary church sends an unhealthy message to pre-Christians by how we practice our faith. We passively communicate, *If you will get up early on your only day off, come to a strange place with strange people, sing strange songs, learn to speak a strange language, and make your kids act in strange ways, we will welcome you to our church.* In short, we expect the pre-Christian to become the missionary! If the contemporary church is going to be effective in fulfilling God's vision, we must stop demanding pre-Christians to do all the work. We must do the hoop-jumping and adjusting and shifting. Debbie authentically became a missionary to reach Jenee.

From the beginning, Debbie had planned to follow up with Jenee. Remember her prayers that God would help her take more initiative to make disciples of those the church reached through its many ministries. You and I—if Jesus is our Savior and Lord—are also called, equipped, and sent to be missionaries everywhere we go. Plan and expect to follow up before you even begin outreach or evangelism of any sort.

You can personally make a disciple—regardless of your personality, your gifts, your skill set, your age, your energy level, or anything else! Remember who God is and the tools he has given us for the mission.

My prayer for each reader is that you will make a commitment to make a disciple this upcoming year. Remember that it is not a matter of skill but of will!

Let's get busy building the kingdom, inviting people into abundant life, and causing heaven to celebrate! Let's, by all means, win some!

Join me and many others as we go and make disciples of all nations!

Questions for New Disciple Makers

1. When have you experienced the deepening of a friendship gradually, over time, the way my friendship with Jackie developed?

2. Did you feel led by the Spirit to invite that person to church?

3. If not, how might you need to pray about God opening your heart to the leading of the Spirit?

4. When was the last time you rearranged your schedule and existing commitments in order to invest relationally in the life of a perfect stranger, the way Debbie did for Jenee?

5. How can you be more sensitive to the Spirit's leading in this way?

TWO

TELLING GOD'S STORY
THROUGH *YOU!*

Evangelism, discipleship, and outreach are words that take on new meanings in almost every generation. Today in Christian circles, using the word "evangelism" can have the same effect as turning on a light in a roach-infested room: believers scatter out of fear. The word "discipleship" may conjure other thoughts, such as sitting in Bible study, Sunday school, or a small group gathering to discuss the Bible with friends. Too often it's the same friends who have been in the same group for years. They rarely reach out to invite anyone new to join their group. Outreach, like evangelism and discipleship, is no exception. The word "outreach" takes me back to the late 1970s, when we went out on Saturday mornings to knock on doors in the neighborhood to invite people to church on Sunday.

Other words that may have lost their impact come to mind when discussing the idea of bringing people to Jesus, such as witnessing and sharing the gospel. I like Jesus's words in Matthew 28:19: "Go and make disciples." We know these words as the Great Commission.

Evangelist missionary to China Hudson Taylor said something that should be obvious to every believer: "The Great Commission is not an option to be considered; it is a command to be obeyed." In other words, the Great Commission is not a suggestion. This book is singularly focused on how to practically implement the command to "go and make disciples." It is amazing how complicated we can make it when Jesus's command was very simple: "Go and make disciples." He continued, ". . . of all nations [all people groups], baptizing them in the name of the Father and of the Son and of the Holy Spirit, and teaching them to obey everything I have commanded you" (Matthew 28:19b–20a). Let's begin by drilling down into the first part: *Go and make disciples.*

I begin by sharing my own story of coming to the faith because it illustrates the simplicity of the Great Commission and how making a disciple can happen when Jesus's command is obeyed.

Like many youth in the seventies, I was on the wrong side of the Jesus Revolution. The telltale signs were all there: long hair down to the middle of my back, worn-out blue jeans, and a daily pursuit of the next careless good time that led many friends in my circles to youthful deaths. Each loss pressed me, even if only briefly, to consider eternity. It was almost as if God were preparing me for something—I just didn't know what. All I knew was that, at each tragic funeral, I had to wrestle with the idea of whether there was a God—and if there wasn't, why even bother? In those days, when a young person passed tragically because of nefarious causes, a thick atmosphere swept across the funeral services, in effect triggering those in attendance to consider where they would spend eternity.

It must've been clear to everyone looking on that my chosen lifestyle could not end well. Social influences, peer pressure, and the drive to fit in blinded me—and most of my friends—from being able to see this inevitability. Yet the evidence was plain; it seemed like everyone I knew was dying. There was a morbid sense that, from my perspective, it was only a matter of time before I would succumb to a similar fate. I found myself going deeper into the use of drugs that numbed my awareness of the inevitability of mortality and eternity, and that method worked for a few years. But at age seventeen, I had an encounter that changed it all.

It was the summer of 1976 on the eastern coast of Virginia. I was a misguided, untethered young man. That July morning, my girlfriend and I had gone to Virginia Beach for the day. After a steady, five-day binge high on four-way hits of blotter acid (a type of LSD that was fairly common in the late seventies), my mind was foggy from the hallucinogenic drug. My body was exhausted from having gone without sleep for several days. At that point in my life, I was beginning to suffer the negative consequences of many bad choices. My short-term memory had already been affected by the smoking of marijuana that began at age twelve.

I will never forget my first experience with marijuana. I had been invited by my brother to visit some of his friends. As we sat there, a little hand-rolled cigarette was passed around. When it came to me, I took a drag and began to feel the calming and relaxing sensation it brought. I loved it, which began a journey into almost daily usage that led to many other drugs—a stronger version of pot, then hash, and finally LSD. I was drinking a lot of alcohol, using way too many illegal drugs, and making bad relational decisions.

After a few hours on the beach that summer day, it was time for lunch. I headed to a boardwalk hamburger joint to get food for my girlfriend and myself. The next thing that happened was a strange encounter with a Jesus Revolution dude. He stopped me and said he had two questions he would like to ask me.

First he asked, "Do you know Jesus?"

It was a question that instantly generated an angry response. "I didn't come here to talk about Jesus, I came here to get a burger. Get out of my face."

As I turned to walk away, the young man courageously—and with a strange, compassionate love I had never experienced—grabbed my elbow and spun me back to face him.

Now, in the part of town where I grew up, people didn't put their hands on strangers without a violent response. That was the first natural response I felt, but it was instantly outmatched by a strange feeling of peace as I looked into the man's eyes. I had to stop and listen. I was almost paralyzed by the next words out of his mouth.

He said, "The Bible says, 'Wide is the gate that leads to destruction, and many people find it, but narrow is the gate that leads to life, and only a few people find it.'" Then he asked, "Are you going to be one of the few who enters the narrow gate to heaven?"

At this, my anger raged again. As he asked the second question, my days-long LSD high instantly evaporated. Now completely sober, paralyzed, and shocked at the impact the question had on my entire being, those words penetrated areas of my soul that had long since become numb to such emotions. The very words of God had cut deep.

In that moment I unleashed a litany of words that would embarrass a drunken sailor. I was furious that this brief encounter had left me sober and therefore more cognizant of my current life choices, the related consequences, and the end that could result. I turned away and headed for the exit, forgetting completely about the hunger in my belly and that my girlfriend was waiting for lunch. My verbal rant continued in my departure from the brief conversation.

I stopped before leaving, turned back and pointed an accusatory finger, and said, "Thanks, buddy—you just ruined my day."

Upon leaving, the reality hit me: this encounter had exposed my spiritual condition. For the first time in my life, it was obvious to me that my spiritual condition was ugly. I somehow at that moment understood the response of the Samaritan woman after Jesus revealed how much he knew about her life. She said to the people of her town, "Come, see a man who told me everything I ever did" (John 4:29). It was as if every wrong thing I had ever done bombarded my mind all at the same time. That encounter ended the day at the beach for me. I was sober, stunned, angry, and confused.

After we gathered our beach gear, we headed to the car for a forty-five-minute drive to Newport News, where I dropped off my girlfriend and then went home myself. I couldn't get there fast enough. It was as if everything in my life up to that moment became a total blur. My every thought was about the inevitable results of my life choices thus far. The fun of the sun, the beach, the LSD trip, and everything else that had mattered to me a mere hour earlier had evaporated like a mist. It was as if the world I knew had just ended and I had to decide which world I would step into for the rest of my life.

I went upstairs to the attic living space where my three brothers and I spent most of our nights. While lying on my back and looking up to heaven, prayers emerged for the first time in many years. My first prayer was something like, "God if you are real, let me know. If you are not real, why should I care about any of this?" As I prayed, I remembered that I had stuffed a religious tract in the pocket of a pair of jeans some weeks earlier. I had found it on top of a toilet in some gas station restroom somewhere. I thought maybe this tract could help me sort out some of the crazy thoughts that were running through my head.

I found the jeans, and the tract, titled, "This Was Your life," was still there. It was the same one I used later in my first disciple-making encounter. It was a cartoon-like story of a man who lived a wicked life and faced the consequences.

"How can I change my life path?" I asked myself.

The last page of the tract offered a few simple steps:

1. Admit you are a sinner.
2. Be willing to turn from your sin.
3. Believe that Jesus died to take away your sins.
4. Pray to invite Jesus to come into your life and change your heart.

I followed the steps, and in an instant, the fear of judgment and my regrets lifted away as the promise of a better life moving forward flooded my soul. I felt free, released, hopeful, and at peace all at the same time. My life changed—both in that moment and in the days that followed.

One of my first actions was to go to the little barber shop where my father had been cutting hair for many years. After I sat down in the chair, Dad began cutting all the hair off. I had not been in the chair of my father's barber shop for years. My hair had become, in some ways, my identity. Growing out my hair had been one of my acts of defiance (a common display of rebellion in those days). Of course, there is nothing wrong with long hair! But it had become a problem for me because it had become my identity. I soon learned—and continue to this day to be reminded—that anything in which I claim identity other than Christ is a form of idolatry. The only thing that mattered to me that day was beginning a new life. And this time, I had a companion, a guide, and a helper to lead me to a better, more productive, less selfish way of being.

My Christian journey began when I was seventeen, almost eighteen. I was an eighth-grade dropout, a recovering drug user, a previous alcoholic, a thief, and a womanizer. My new identity was only in Christ, and it has been the single most important identity of my life from that day until today, almost fifty years later.

I wasn't very far into my new life before I recognized that I was way behind the curve in Christian development. I had little to offer the Christian world. In fact, in *my* estimation, my contribution capacity was negative. There was not much to work with, but I had a new start.

As I reflect now on my new life in Christ I am reminded of the parable of the sower. Some call it the parable of the soils. It can be found in Matthew 13. The seed in my story would be the word from Matthew 7:13–14 the young man at the beach boardwalk had shared with me that day. I myself was the soil. It has occurred to me often that most Christians would not have seen me as good soil. We tend to judge soil before we sow into it, only investing seed in what appears to be good soil. This parable has become a rich passage for me. Almost daily, God's Spirit reminds me to be ready to scatter the seed of his Word everywhere—even in places that, by every visible indicator, appear to be bad soil. That is what is so marvelous about Jesus's story. Austerity was not, and is not, God's view of seed scattering. How grateful I am that the young man scattered the seed of the Word of God into my heart that day.

There are a few important reasons I began this book with my story. Most importantly, the story is a reminder that the making of disciples is accomplished by the *work of God*, through the *obedience* of a believer *sharing* the Word of God with a *pre-Christian*. As we study disciple making, it is imperative to know God has commissioned all believers to do this important work. We can't do it without him and the gifts he has provided. He did, however, commission all of us who are the people of God to do the work of disciple making. It is his divine plan to save the entire world. It is still his will that none perish.

The tragedy of the Christian world I live in is that only the gifted, the special, and the aggressive sense the need to be involved in disciple making. My story of salvation *should* be common—but it's an anomaly. My prayer is that every believer who reads this book will become a disciple whom God can use in the same way he used that young man at the beach to guide me to faith. That young man never knew the life-changing impact he had on me that day, and similarly, we may never know the full extent of the impact we have on others—but God knows.

Questions for New Disciple Makers

1. Are pre-Christians coming to faith through my life?

2. If not, why not?

3. What can I do to change this reality?

4. What are the tools provided to me to get the work of the Great Commission done?

5. Who should respond to the Great Commission?

6. How does the average believer start the disciple-making journey?

7. How do I start conversations that might lead to faith?

8. How do I pursue the fulfillment of the Great Commission while avoiding the pitfall of seeing pre-Christian people as a project?

9. How can an introvert be an effective disciple maker?

10. Why should I want abundant life for all?

11. When have I sensed God nudging me into someone's life?

THREE

SIX MYTHS THAT HINDER DISCIPLE MAKING

We demolish arguments and every pretension that sets itself up against the knowledge of God, and we take captive every thought to make it obedient to Christ.

—*2 Corinthians 10:5*

When we think about disciple making, we all carry preconceived ideas that can block our ability to share our faith effectively. This chapter examines six myths that have hindered the spread of the gospel.

Myth #1: I am all alone in my disciple-making journey.

God's saving grace is always ahead of us. The Bible teaches about the grace that goes before us. Paul addresses it in Romans 5:8: "But God demonstrates his own love for us in this: While we were still sinners, Christ died for us." Jesus addresses it in John 4:38: "I sent you to reap what you have not worked for. Others have done the hard work, and you have reaped the benefits of their labor." Jeremiah 29:11 addresses God's working for our future: "'For I know the plans I have for you, declares the LORD, 'plans to prosper you and not to harm you, plans to give you a hope and a future.'"

When we encounter pre-Christians, we must remember that God has promised to go before us. God's prevenient grace in my own pre-Christian life was evident. Just over a year before my encounter at the beach, my older brother Allen and I had a conversation about eternity. Allen passed away at age twenty-one in a car accident mere months after this discussion about eternal things, which happened following a Bob Harrington Crusade.

We hooligans had planned to go and see what a chaplain from the dregs of Bourbon Street in New Orleans was like. We thought we were going to see a circus, a show of religious weirdness. Well, the joke was on me. I left the crusade under deep, heavy conviction. I was, at the time, living with Allen and his wife, Susan. When I returned to the apartment, I asked Allen a serious question. I had been afraid to be vulnerable with my buddies. Their friendship wasn't the type that would tolerate vulnerability and fear. My personal feelings would reek of weakness and lead to bullying and humiliation, so instead I addressed my spiritual questions to my older brother. I will never forget his response. It impacted me in a way nothing had before.

He said, "Mark, you are thinking real clear, man. Serving God is the right thing. Don't blow it like I have. I'm sowing a few wild oats now, but I plan to get into a good place with God before I turn forty." Well, only a month or two later, his earthly life ended.

Allen's death impacted me so much that I couldn't forget his words. At his funeral, I kept hearing them over and over again. I believe one of the reasons for my violent response to the man at the beach was that I knew Allen had probably not had time to make things right with God. And the words of my friend at the beach were, "Are you going to be one of the few who makes it to heaven?" That, I am convinced, was God's prevenient grace in my life.

To clarify, God did not kill my brother. Allen didn't die so I could become a Christian. I do, however, believe that God used my grief and my experience to prepare me for the beach encounter. God perfectly prepared my mind and heart for that moment. When I heard those words, "Are you going to be one of the few?" I was undone.

A truth that is evident in Scripture and the nature of God is that he doesn't want even one person to perish but is waiting and hopeful for all to repent. As 2 Peter 3:9 says, "The Lord is not slow in keeping his promise, as some understand slowness. Instead he is patient with you, not wanting anyone to perish, but everyone to come to repentance."

The best prescription for fear when approaching a pre-Christian with the gospel is the certainty that the Spirit has preceded us. God still seeks to save the lost. Romans 1:18–20 has been a great fear buster in my own disciple-making endeavors:

The wrath of God is being revealed from heaven against all the godlessness and wickedness of people, who suppress the truth by their wickedness, since what may be known about God is plain to them, because God has made it plain to them. For since the creation of the world God's invisible qualities—his eternal power and divine nature—have been clearly seen, being understood from what has been made, so that people are without excuse.

As you begin thinking about becoming a disciple maker, remember that God has gone before you. His prevenient grace—the grace that prepares pre-Christians for an encounter with God—is doing the work ahead of you.

Myth #2: I don't see immediate fruit, so I must not be doing it right.

Beware of the temptation to judge your disciple-making effectiveness by what you see with your physical eyes. That young man at Virginia Beach had no clue what had happened in my life up to that point. The same is true with you and me when we encounter a stranger or begin a new friendship that we hope leads to faith.

He had no awareness of the personal losses of close friends, family, and neighbors that had occurred in the previous year or so of my life. God knew of those things, though. He could not have engineered a more appropriate approach with me than: "Are you going to be one of the few who will make it through the narrow gate?" But the Holy Spirit did.

Because of my hostility in response to him, that young man most likely left our encounter frustrated, feeling like a failure, defeated, and determined that the effort had been fruitless and certainly a bad idea. I imagine he may have been tempted to say, like so many believers, "Well I tried the personal evangelism stuff, and it doesn't work." Or, as so many have said to me at evangelism training events across North America, "Personal evangelism is just not for me."

I hear stories almost weekly of those who remember their first evangelism encounter that went south. Those experiences are often misinterpreted as failure. My experience certainly would have been interpreted that way by the young man at the beach—yet it was the very encounter that turned my whole life around. Don't stop just because you had what appeared to be a bad experience! I sure hope that man at the beach didn't stop.

Myth #3: Quick encounters of gospel presentations are ineffective.

We have all heard the horror stories of hit-and-run evangelism. It has been used in Christian comedy routines and made fun of in Christian circles. I think this myth comes from a good place. We do hope to have a long-term relational impact on the people to whom we minister. The best chance to show someone how the goodness of God can positively impact their lives is through a solid relationship over a period of time. Yet we must not underestimate small beginnings (see Zechariah 4:10).

Remember that Jesus had a brief encounter with a man on the cross. The result was, "Today you will be with me in paradise" (Luke 23:43). We tend to forget that God can take something small and make it impactful. My story of faith was catalyzed by a brief encounter. I have replayed that experience at the boardwalk burger joint in my mind many times. As I go over it, I am sure the entire incident lasted no longer than three minutes, but the impact was eternal.

Philip's encounter with the Ethiopian eunuch was brief, yet many African believers trace their Christian heritage back to that very interaction. Interestingly, the Holy Spirit whisked Philip away immediately after their short conversation and the eunuch's baptism. Jesus's encounter with the woman at the well was brief, yet it led to many in her city coming to faith.

The danger in this myth is that we underestimate God's power to take something small and make it impactful. We used to sing a song in my early days of faith, "Little is much when God is in it." I believe that to be true.

We should be careful when criticizing any style of evangelism that has worked to bring people to faith. I have heard speakers criticize the four spiritual laws because they met someone who resisted coming to church due to a bad experience with that tactic. The truth is that thousands of people have come to faith as a result of this method of sharing the gospel.

One thing I have learned in my half century of church and Christian engagement about the church and Christians is that we are very good at deconstructing every method of evangelism ever used. We are, however, not as good at practicing effective methods. We should do our best to establish long-term relationships with those whom we are loving into the kingdom, but we must guard against making light of small beginnings. The Great Commission is to make disciples. Often the first practical step is evangelism to those who have not yet believed. So we must be involved in evangelism at some level if we are going to make disciples.

Myth #4: Only those with the gift of evangelism can be effective at disciple making.

In Ephesians 4:11–13, Paul tells the Ephesians that the gift of evangelism was given to some so that they may equip the rest of the church in evangelism. There is no evidence in this text that the gifted evangelist would be the most active of all believers in doing evangelism. One could make a strong argument here that the primary praxis of those who have the gift is to give it away to the rest of the church.

I am convinced that many believers today read this text to mean there should be super-apostles, super-evangelists, and more, who would manage that specific work while other believers watched from a spectator posture. Yet a good reading of the entire text could lead us to the conclusion that every believer should have some measure of all the gifts. Those gifted with these fivefold ministries were given more for *equipping* than for exclusively doing the practice of the gift.

It is interesting because, in every professional occupation, we know that to be successful, we must get training, develop skills, and even experience failure so we can become the best we can be in that field. It seems only in the conversation about disciple making do we draw a line at gifting. Just because something is difficult, uncomfortable, challenging, risky, or even dangerous, that doesn't mean we shouldn't develop skills and proficiency at it. According to Jesus in Acts 1:8, the only qualifier for being a witness is to have the Holy Spirit. Well, every believer has the Holy Spirit. Therefore, every believer is equipped to witness. Not everyone is particularly gifted in evangelism, but we all have the calling to make disciples.

This idea reminds me of my first full-time job for a tree-trimming company. I started as a ground man, otherwise known by the more experienced in the crew as a "ground grunt." That meant I had to cut, pile, and drag brush from one place to another all day long, often for hundreds of feet at a time. Once the brush was delivered next to the chipper, the next-level ground person took over. This person ran the chipper. These machines make the loud whining sound of turning entire trees into mulch. When they are running, everyone for blocks can hear.

I was afraid of the chipper and would have been perfectly content to stay a ground grunt—but then I was told, "If you don't learn to use the chipper, you will not stay employed here very long." Wow, that was frightening. The more experienced workers (the climbers and the foreman) used to tell the rookie ground grunts stories at lunch about foolish chipper operators who became tangled and caught up in the brush and were pulled into the chipper. I won't tell you the rest of the folklore. It became graphic and gory. That was how they prepared us to move into that role? Really? Yes, that was the initiation conversation. They were trying to teach us to respect and have a healthy fear of the dangers of the chipper. Knowing this would make us better at the job.

It wasn't long before I became a chipper operator. Soon I was comfortable running it. I became so good at it, it was almost second nature. I no longer feared the chipper. Then, I was asked to put on climbing gear and learn to be a climber. As I practiced, learned, and developed my skills, I became quite a tree surgeon. That was the apex of freedom. I made it to the top of my profession (no pun intended)—not because I was naturally gifted but because I trained, learned, listened, and practiced until I overcame the fear and worked through the worries and angst associated with it.

Disciple making involves much the same process. To become good disciple makers, we must face our fears and move headlong into the risks, worries, and objections we most certainly will face as we obey the Great Commission—not because we want to keep a job, like I did with my tree-trimming responsibilities, but because Jesus rose from the grave for lost and broken people who need to hear—maybe from you—the great story of salvation.

Another way to debunk this common myth is to remember that scary things often lose their punch the more familiar they become. In 1975, I began the journey of learning how to drive a car. It was ugly. I failed the driving test two times before I passed. I knew the law! I just didn't understand *why* a person had to stop fully at a stop sign when it was clear nothing was coming. It seemed inefficient to me. Well, the guy grading me on the test was pretty clear. Until I completely stopped at all stop signs, I would not pass. Finally, on the third try, I learned the lesson.

My stop-sign troubles soon paled in significance when I began driving on highways. My greatest fear was that I would get in heavy traffic at high speeds surrounded by other cars on both sides and accidentally swerve. I couldn't fathom how everyone stayed in their lanes all at the same time. I reasoned that I would simply only drive on one-lane roads for the rest of my life. That would take care of that issue!

My Driver's Education teacher gave me a tip: "Mark, there is a center point on the hood of most cars." He noticed there was one on the 1970 Oldsmobile Delta 88 I had learned to drive in. He said, "If you line that center point on the hood with the white line on the right side of the road, you will stay in your lane, no problem." That sounded pretty good to me. It was a miracle; I stayed in my lane on the highway with an intense focus on that line and my center point. The funny thing was, after a few weeks of driving, I automatically stopped focusing on the hood ornament and became comfortable driving with my newly learned instincts of staying in my lane. I was reminded of this experience not too long ago as I drove through the city of Atlanta. There were six to eight lanes of traffic, and I didn't even have to think about staying in my lane. It had become intuitive and natural.

We all *learn* to be good at things through training, practicing, failing or making mistakes, and trying again. We simply need to apply that principle to disciple making, witnessing, and outreach. Start with baby steps.

Step 1: Begin praying daily, *"Lord, help me to have a broken heart for the same things that break your heart."*

Step 2: Begin prayer driving in a neighborhood where you have a heart connection. Just start there. Think of it as a hood ornament. You probably will not become a great disciple maker overnight, but you can begin to develop good habits that will develop into fearless disciple making one day!

Step 3: Begin prayer *walking* (instead of driving) to get closer to real people, and maybe God will open an opportunity to start a conversation and maybe a relationship that could lead to developing faith.

Myth #5: I am introverted and timid, so God doesn't expect me to be a disciple maker.

If most contemporary spokespeople for disciple-making styles are correct, then relational discipleship is the best method—which puts introverts at the top of the gifting list! Introverts are often more effective at developing deep, long-term relationships than extroverts. Introverts are excellent at listening, and listening is key to any solid long-term relationship. Believe me, I have been married to the same woman for more than forty years, and I can testify that listening is the key to us staying happily together. I have learned to listen to my wife and understand what makes her happy, fulfilled, sad, engaged, and more. The listening aspect is one reason I am convinced that introverts may be better at relational evangelism that leads to disciple making than extroverts. The only difference is that extroverts need to learn to listen (which takes discipline) while introverts need to learn to speak (which is difficult and takes discipline as well).

All believers need to reread Paul: "For God has not given us a spirit of timidity, but of power and love and discipline" (2 Timothy 1:7, NASB). There Scripture goes again, telling us we receive power when we receive the Spirit—not just to be witnesses but also to overcome timidity with the instincts of the Spirit to speak the Word of God boldly. Acts 8:1 says, "On that day a great persecution broke out against the church in Jerusalem, and all except the apostles were scattered throughout Judea and Samaria." Notice that the laity were scattered! The text doesn't separate the scattered introverts from the scattered extroverts. They are all lumped into one group—"all except the Apostles."

Natural timidity is overshadowed by the Spirit in our lives, as are many other natural instincts. We tend to forget that when we receive the Spirit we receive power to be witnesses. Power is not from our natural instincts. Our natural instincts are overwhelmed by the Spirit's instincts. When we receive the Spirit, we become like Jesus. We inherit his spirit, his nature, his power, his peace—his everything.

Myth #6: The current culture is not a good environment for disciple making.

This myth is leading many to completely disengage from evangelism, witnessing, and disciple making, but guess what? There's never been a culture where it was easy to evangelize, witness, and make disciples. The first-century Christians certainly didn't have a good environment for it—yet look at how God grew his church in that culture. Places where the gospel is most suppressed, seem to be the places where the greatest expansion of the kingdom has been experienced.

Tertullian said, "The blood of the martyrs was the seed of the church"—not because of their natural gifting of evangelism and not because they had an easy start but because they were determined to bring the world to Jesus, even if it meant suffering horrible deaths in coliseums, on crosses, or by stoning. They "loved not their lives unto death." Paul gives a picture of this mindset in 2 Corinthians 11:23–27:

> Are they servants of Christ? (I am out of my mind to talk like this.) I am more. I have worked much harder, been in prison more frequently, been flogged more severely, and been exposed to death again and again. Five times I received from the Jews the forty lashes minus one. Three times I was beaten with rods, once I was pelted with stones, three times I was shipwrecked, I spent a night and a day in the open sea, I have been constantly on the move. I have been in danger from rivers, in danger from bandits, in danger from my fellow Jews, in danger from Gentiles; in danger in the city, in danger in the country, in danger at sea; and in danger from false believers. I have labored and toiled and have often gone without sleep; I have known hunger and thirst and have often gone without food; I have been cold and naked.

That sounds like a pretty gospel-friendly environment, right?!

In the Christian culture of North America, we tend to resist sharing our faith if it might somehow cross a line of social mores or cultural norms. We are even fearful of using more passive methods, let alone more direct methods. Too many Christians are more concerned that we used the wrong nomenclature than they are that people are living without Jesus. It seems outrageous to many today to approach a stranger like Philip did, like Paul did, like Jonah did, like Jesus did. How rude to speak to a stranger about your faith!

Paul addressed this problem with a dose of reality therapy. He says in 2 Corinthians 2:15–16 (NKJV), "For we are to God the fragrance of Christ among those who are being saved and among those who are perishing. To the one we are the aroma of death leading to death, and to the other the aroma of life leading to life. And who is sufficient for these things?" The fear of cultural pushback and social rejection is a powerful weapon to stop the spread of the gospel. Regardless of the method used, the enemy of bringing the world to Jesus is very busy making Christians afraid of cultural suppression.

Any style of evangelism that brings Jesus as the answer to the fallenness of our world will initiate reprisals. We need to remember, as is indicated by the statistics on page 67 from Lifeway Research, that people are more interested in Jesus and the gospel than most of us assume. People know their need for God. *Any* method we use will be rejected by some and accepted by others. That has always been the case. It is helpful to remember, as we pursue the Great Commission, that Augustine said, "Our hearts are restless until they find their rest in you." And Pascal: "Everyone has a god-shaped vacuum that only God can fill." People are more ready for spiritual conversations than we think.

There never was and never will be a time when living out the gospel is *always* met with joy and enthusiasm.

Was Jesus a loving person? Absolutely!

Was Jesus compassionate? Of course!

Was Jesus gracious? Certainly!

Was Jesus the embodiment of perfect love? Absolutely!

Did Jesus do or say anything that wasn't God's perfect will? Never!

So why did they persecute him and then murder him on a cross after only three years of ministry? Because, to those who are in the process of perishing, Jesus's way of living comes off as a stench of death. The gospel is often resisted and rejected at first.

In Matthew 14 we read the story of John the Baptist's beheading after he spoke up and provoked Herodias: "Now Herod had arrested John and bound him and put him in prison because of Herodias, his brother Philip's wife, for John had been saying to him: 'It is not lawful for you to have her'" (vv. 3–4).

Why did John the Baptist suffer a beheading? Was it because he was too aggressive? It doesn't sound too far-fetched to see the future church respond to people like John in this fashion. "Decaf, John! Take a chill pill, bro. Don't be so direct. Come on, man, couldn't you have told the truth with more love? You didn't have to be so judgmental. You need a class on anger management." I know that sounds extreme, but it's an example of how we tend to drift into thinking we can somehow reach a fallen culture without truth and love.

Try though we might, we will probably never attain the high measures of love, grace, compassion, and obedience to the Father that Jesus reached. We could say the same thing about many New Testament characters. Most of them way further perfected the fulfillment of the mission of Christ than we have. Why were they so hated?

Are we arrogant enough to assume we could somehow be effective in fulfilling God's mission without opposition, pushback, or rejection? It seems there is a shift in the current culture to a type of Christianity that could become that arrogant. Often I wonder if one day the church in North America will figure out how to do our faith without opposition. It's simple—just don't share our faith, and don't offend anyone! We may not fulfill the Great Commission, but at least everyone will think we are nice people!

The reality is that we are in an environment that is much more friendly toward and knowledgeable of the church than we might imagine. In 2023, Lifeway Research discovered the following positive results that might surprise you.

- 59 percent of Americans believe hell is a real place and certain people will be punished for eternity
- 64 percent of Americans believe there will come a day when Jesus will return as a judge for all peple who have ever lived
- 57 percent of Americans believe righteousness before God comes through faith in Jesus, not by personal effort
- 64 percent of Americans believe the only way sin can be forgiven is through Jesus's sacrificial death
- 60 percent of Americans believe God's gift of salvation is only available to those who trust in Jesus alone as their Savior

As we continue to discuss disciple making, remember that our culture today may be much more receptive to the good news than we think! Whatever the situation, it is absolutely essential that we never use methods of disciple making that mock other cultures or are disrespectful to anyone. At the same time, we must never forget that even those who were full of grace, full of the Holy Spirit, and full of wisdom (see Jesus and Stephen) could face certain opposition from those who are in the process of perishing. Even with the best intention, methods, and grace, the gospel itself is what many find offensive. The gospel is the problem that makes us think our culture is not a good fit.

As we dive deeper into disciple-making practices, let's make sure our methods are as kind and gracious as those of Jesus. Yet we should anticipate that the gospel, regardless of how well it is presented, will often be met with cultural resistance. Accepting this as true will help prepare us for when it does happen. The proper solution to cultural resistance to the gospel is not to do it without telling the truth in love. We must do both.

Questions for New Disciple Makers

1. Which of the myths mentioned in this chapter is most likely to cause you to avoid sharing your faith?

2. What objection to disciple making do you struggle with that maybe was not covered in this chapter?

3. What actions could you take to overcome the myth you struggle with?

4. How could you avoid embracing some of the myths as you move forward in your Christian faith? How would 2 Corinthians 10:5 inform this response?

5. What practices and behaviors could you engage in to avoid the myths that might hinder your own disciple-making journey?

FOUR

PRAYER AND DISCIPLE MAKING

I will make a bold and brash statement to start this chapter: it is not possible for someone to have a healthy prayer life without being missional.

By "healthy," I mean a prayer life that is two-way—prayer where there is as much *listening* to God as there is *talking* to God. I learned the importance of listening to God early in my faith development, in one of my first lead pastor roles. I was green, but I wanted to do everything right. I was focused on making everyone in the church happy while simultaneously investing in pre-Christian people in the community.

One morning I rose early, which has been my habit now for most of my ministry life. I learned that between four o'clock and nine o'clock in the morning are the most uninterrupted hours of the day, so those became my time to be alone with God and his Word. For the first time, I had committed that morning to spend an hour praying. I was excited and ready to pray for an entire hour, and to repeat the practice one day every week for the rest of my ministry. I was not going to be that disciple who could not watch and pray with Jesus for one hour (see Matthew 26:40)!

In preparation for this new prayer covenant, I purchased one of those old manual alarm clocks that was round with the two bells and a hammer on top that would bang each bell when the alarm went off. I had a list of prayer requests and a list of praises to pray over. At the top of that list was a new Christian family that weighed heavily on my mind. The father, Johnny, had become a Christian only a month earlier and had been sober for thirty days. Johnny had abused alcohol his entire life. I went to the sanctuary, put some good Christian worship music on in the background, set the alarm for one hour, and began.

I went through the list of praises first, then through the list of requests, spending most of that request time praying for the new family struggling with deliverance from alcohol. I celebrated Johnny's thirty-day sobriety and thanked God for how he'd been working in Johnny's life and the life of Johnny's entire family. I prayed for Johnny's wife, who had not yet made a commitment to Christ. I wept over Johnny and his family. I prayed for every attender of my new church. I prayed for the businesses in the community. I prayed for my family—my wife, my children, my brothers and sisters. I prayed for the government—city, state and federal.

By this time, I felt as though I had been praying for hours. That crazy manual alarm must be broken. I looked at the clock, and it had only been a few minutes. I was surprised and embarrassed before my Lord. Then it occurred to me that I had not yet learned how to be in the presence of God without an agenda. I finally relaxed and began, maybe for the first time, to actually have a conversation with God.

Most of my prayers prior to this had been more about worrying about my requests and strategizing how to fix them, or using the time to make personal plans on how to fix the issues I brought to God. I began to feel the weight of personal guilt that my previous prayer times had been more about begging for help, strategizing, worrying, and planning than they had been about enhancing my relationship with my heavenly Father. Starting again (I had fifty minutes left to do it right), I begged forgiveness for approaching God as my go-to problem solver, rather than as a friend and companion to help navigate life and ministry together.

That day I learned the most important lesson from God. Prayer is a conversation with God—with him doing most of the talking and me doing most of the listening. I discovered that if I spent time listening, God would give direction, guidance, and counsel on how to navigate the challenges of life and ministry.

Out of that first healthy prayer time, I was certain I had to go and visit Johnny, the thirty-days-sober alcoholic whose wife had not yet accepted Christ. I had been given a clear mission to accomplish. God gave me clear direction. He sent me out of that prayer time with a purpose and a plan: go visit Johnny and encourage him and his wife in their new faith journey. Listening in prayer led me to do mission.

Prior to this experience, my prayer life had been more therapeutic than practical. Previous prayer times had left me feeling good that I'd had some alone time with God, when actually those times were more me time than they were us time. Prayer had become downtime for me to work through, without interruption, problems God wanted desperately to help me with—but I never gave him the opportunity to tell me how. I was too busy strategizing and planning rather than listening.

I had an epiphany. Maybe my giving God a list of things for him to fix in my life and ministry wasn't as important for the kingdom as God giving *me* a list of missions I was to accomplish for *him*. This idea revolutionized my prayer life. I discovered that God has a mission for me that is more important than the mission I wanted God to help me with. I knew that my plans and dreams mattered to God. However, I had not considered in any sincere way that God has plans and dreams for me and my life and for the lives of those he has asked me to reach and love into the kingdom.

I immediately rose from this first hour of prayer and headed out to pursue the mission I had been given to go visit Johnny and his family, encourage them in the faith, and pray with them. As I left, I noticed a sticky note I had made the night before and stuck to the corner of my desk reminding me that one of the most influential families in the church had a son who was suffering with the flu. Although I had a divine imperative directly from God to go visit Johnny, I decided I could stop on my way and visit this family. What would it hurt? I could kill two birds with one stone. The side trip would take fewer than twenty minutes. What would twenty minutes matter to Johnny's family? They were probably still in bed anyway.

So I put on my "noble Christian" hat and went to visit the family with the sick kid. It went well. It was nice. I prayed for the lad, then headed to accomplish the mission I had been clearly given in prayer. When I arrived, I was shocked to find that Johnny had, just a few minutes earlier, purchased his first six-pack of beer in thirty days and was well on his way to getting drunk.

Johnny asked me, "Pastor, where were you? I needed you. I was being tempted so bad and prayed that God would send someone to help me over and through the temptation. No one came. I did it. I started drinking again."

Johnny never, to my knowledge, stopped drinking after that.

Somehow, I knew that my decisions that day (although it seemed like a small thing to me) had some bearing on Johnny's deliverance—or lack thereof. I wondered if putting my "noble Christian" instinct ahead of the divine imperative was disobedience. Was it possible that such a small decision could affect so large an outcome?

I then began to reflect on my personal story. Is it possible that the young man who met me and shared the truth in 1976 was set up by God for that moment and that place? Is it possible that, if God's will were obeyed by his people every time, his vision that none would perish (see Matthew 18:14; 2 Peter 3:9) could be accomplished? My experience leads me to ask these questions:

1. Is it possible that God is constantly setting up scenarios, situations, and opportunities for his people to impact the lives of pre-Christians?

2. Is it possible that the redemption of the world depends on God but is also somehow connected to our obedience?

3. Could my disobedience impact the ability of others to live abundantly in Jesus's grace?

4. Is God constantly working and trying to orchestrate lives in such ways that the world could be saved if all Christians walked in obedience?

I will never be able to answer these important questions for myself with any certainty. I do believe that God was definitely trying that day to orchestrate my schedule with the goal of saving Johnny from a life of addiction, and I totally failed to deliver my part of God's divine plan. But I also believe that God was yet capable of saving Johnny despite my own shortcomings, and I pray that he eventually did.

Because we are discussing prayer and disciple making in this chapter, the question becomes, are prayer and obedience more important than we think? Let's look at a few biblical examples.

Moses and the Burning Bush (Exodus 3–4)

This is an amazing passage of scripture. The two chapters take us through a long conversation between God and Moses. God calls Moses to go and deliver God's people from bondage; Moses gives his excuses and reasons why this is not a good idea. God wins the argument, and Moses proceeds to bring the deliverance God promised.

What if Moses had decided it was not convenient for him to go back to Egypt? What if Moses decided he had won the argument and left before God convinced him to follow through? Would the children of Israel have been delivered?

God was orchestrating another miracle. For it to happen, Moses needed to hear and obey God. The result was the deliverance of the people of God from four hundred years of bondage.

Prayer led to mission!

Jonah and the Ninevites (Jonah 1–4)

In this story, God gave Jonah a mission to go and preach in Nineveh. Jonah resisted. God finally won the argument (through a series of incidents that ultimately left Jonah deserted on the beach near Nineveh, after having been swallowed and then spit back up by a large fish). Jonah reluctantly preached to the city. As a result, the entire city repented and turned to God.

What if Jonah had decided not to obey God? Would the Ninevites have been saved?

God was orchestrating another miracle. For it to happen, Jonah needed to hear and obey God. The result was that the entire city of Nineveh turned to God.

Prayer led to mission!

Stephen's Speech to the Sanhedrin (Acts 7)

In Acts, Stephen was a layman who never had a homiletics or hermeneutics class and probably not even a public-speaking class. His job as part of the church was to help end the division between the Hellenistic and Jewish widows in the daily distribution of food. His job was handing out bread—that was all. He took it a step further and performed some signs and wonders that got him arrested and brought in before the Sanhedrin, where he preached a sermon—or, really, a historical overview of the history of God and his people, but there was a twist: he added a few comments at the end that upset the Sanhedrin and cost him his life.

But what if Stephen was God's best hope to reach a young persecutor of Christians named Saul? What if Stephen had thought better of things, had decided to value his life and keep his mouth shut?

Stephen's sermon in Acts 7 reminds me of Myth #5 in chapter 3. Would we have coached Stephen to add the final words of his really good history lesson for the Jewish people? Would we have coached Stephen to conclude with the Isaiah passage and call it a day? I can hear homiletics teachers and contemporary preachers admonishing Stephen: "Quit while you're ahead, bro. You don't have to be so graphic. Did you really need to provoke them like that?"

Look at verses 51–53 in Stephen's speech to the Sanhedrin. This is what he left them with: "You stiff-necked people! Your hearts and ears are still uncircumcised. You are just like your ancestors:

You always resist the Holy Spirit! Was there ever a prophet your ancestors did not persecute? They even killed those who predicted the coming of the Righteous One. And now you have betrayed and murdered him—you who have received the law that was given through angels but have not obeyed it."

The answer is yes, many in the contemporary world would have coached him to drop these final remarks. Stephen's obedience, courage, and boldness did cost him his life, but his words obviously impacted young Saul and contributed to his coming to faith.

What if Stephen had not preached this message? What if the crowd had not been provoked to violence? What if Saul had not witnessed and affirmed his killing? Couldn't God have found some other leader to bring Saul to the precipice of faith?

God was orchestrating another miracle. For it to happen, Stephen needed to obey God and preach a hard sermon. The result was that the greatest evangelist and apostle of all time was saved not long after. One could posit that this experience (watching a Christian die because of his courageous faith) was used in Saul's life as a form of prevenient grace to prepare Saul for his conversion.

Ananias's Obedience (Acts 9)

In Damascus there was a disciple named Ananias. The Lord called to him in a vision, "Ananias!"

"Yes, Lord," he answered.

The Lord told him, "Go to the house of Judas on Straight Street and ask for a man from Tarsus named Saul, for he is praying. In a vision he has seen a man named Ananias come and place his hands on him to restore his sight."

"Lord," Ananias answered, "I have heard many reports about this man and all the harm he has done to your holy people in Jerusalem. And he has come here with authority from the chief priests to arrest all who call on your name."

But the Lord said to Ananias, "Go! This man is my chosen instrument to proclaim my name to the Gentiles and their kings and to the people of Israel. I will show him how much he must suffer for my name."

Then Ananias went to the house and entered it. Placing his hands on Saul, he said, "Brother Saul, the Lord—Jesus, who appeared to you on the road as you were coming here—has sent me so that you may see again and be filled with the Holy Spirit." Immediately, something like scales fell from Saul's eyes, and he could see again. He got up and was baptized, and after taking some food, he regained his strength.

(Acts 9:10–19)

God was orchestrating another miracle—that of Saul becoming Paul and receiving sight and the baptism of the Holy Spirit.

Prayer led to mission!

After Ananias obeyed God, Saul began preaching Jesus in the synagogues, among the very people it had been his mission to persecute just a few days prior. Ananias was another layman who was given a clear directive from God. He resisted at first, sharing with God his objections, but eventually God won the argument, Ananias obeyed, and Saul received sight as well as the Holy Spirit, and began to carry out God's mission for him as an apostle.

This all occurred because an obedient layman said yes to a difficult directive. Think of the weight of God's directive to Ananias. God told him that he had given Saul a vision of Ananias visiting him.

For God's mission to happen, Ananias needed to hear and obey. The result was that the greatest evangelist and apostle of all time was released into the world.

As we read these and many other stories from God's Word, it is easy to say that yes, God would have raised someone else up had these leaders succumbed to their fears, objections, and reasoning over their faith. After all, the Bible and history don't record the stories of those whom God *didn't* use because they said no to God. What we do know is that those we have records of *did* hear God and *did* respond in obedience, and the miraculous happened as a result.

I want to leave you with a few questions to ponder as you think of your prayer life, your obedience, and the possible related consequences.

1. Are you today taking seriously the imperative to take time to hear from God?
2. Has your prayer life become a series of planning and strategizing sessions, with diminishing opportunities to actually hear God's voice and direction on how to reach his lost world?
3. If God were to stop you on a road and redirect you, as he did Philip in Acts 8, when he brought the Ethiopian eunuch to faith, would you hear and obey?
4. Do your prayers lead to mission?

If nothing else, this overview of those who heard from God, obeyed, and saw the miraculous occur as a result should help us understand that our prayer times are the place where God begins to orchestrate his divine redemption through the lives of his people into the lives of those who are not yet his people.

What miraculous missional activity are we missing by taking lightly our time in prayer? Let your heart be touched, your mind inspired, and your life moved to mission as you spend quality time developing a healthy prayer life that will almost assuredly lead you to mission beyond your wildest imagination. "Now to him who is able to do immeasurably more than all we ask or imagine, according to his power that is at work within us, to him be glory in the church and in Christ Jesus throughout all generations, for ever and ever! Amen" (Ephesians 3:20–21).

Questions for New Disciple Makers

1. Is your prayer life leading you to mission, or is it more a time of self-therapy, strategy, and planning?

2. When was the last time in your prayer life that you were certain God was directing you to go and do mission somewhere or in service of someone?

3. Please take ten minutes now to pray. Ask God, *"Is there something you wish me to do for you today?"* Listen with a notepad and pen, and jot down what comes to mind.

FIVE

THE MIRACULOUS SIMPLICITY OF DISCIPLE MAKING

It was a spring Tuesday morning in Gainesville, Florida, about 11:30 a.m. I was off to a meeting with two young people: Shakira (Kira) and Junior (Jun), whom I had only known a short time. Both had attended our new church plant a few times, Kira a few more times than Jun. Both had minimal exposure to our fledgling church—a few Bible studies and a sermon or two. Jun had left his Bible at the location where we met the previous night for Bible study. I had offered to return it Tuesday around lunch. He agreed and offered to bring Kira. The meeting was planned. I had been praying for several weeks for both of them to come to faith and surrender their lives to Jesus.

For context, and to give a better perspective of the meeting, let me give a few details and a little background. At the time, I was a sixty-four-year-old, white, middle-income, five-foot-eight-inch guy who had been serving Jesus since I was almost eighteen. Kira was a sixteen-year-old Black young woman from a single-parent home in a low-income neighborhood. Jun was her older brother—twenty-four, single, and about six feet, two inches. He lived with a relative in an area not far from Kira. I share this information to illustrate the obvious differences in age, socioeconomics, and race because God's Spirit guides us to bridge gaps between ourselves and those whom God calls us to reach and love into his kingdom.

One of the great sins of the contemporary church is segregating people like the rest of the world does. In fact, the church is doing an even worse job than the rest of the world on this measure. We need to catch up and then begin to lead. We tend only to interact with, associate with, and reach out to others in our own homogeneous groups. I sure am grateful Jesus didn't function that way. Philippians 2:3–8 can guide us here:

Do nothing out of selfish ambition or vain conceit. Rather, in humility value others above yourselves, not looking to your own interests but each of you to the interests of the others. In your relationships with one another, have the same mindset as Christ Jesus: Who, being in very nature God, did not consider equality with God something to be used to his own advantage; rather, he made himself nothing by taking the very nature of a servant, being made in human likeness. And being found in appearance as a man, he humbled himself by becoming obedient to death—even death on a cross!

Confession: I have experienced regularly throughout my Christian life the temptation to minister only to those who are like me. God has helped me with this. When I pray, I often sense the Spirit leading me toward those who are not like me, so I try to interact with and reach those whom God directs me to.

Occasionally I ask God, "Why do you keep sending me to people who are nothing like me?"

His response is always, *"My Son was far more different from you than you are from those whom I call you to reach. Love those I send you to, and reach those I call you to reach."*

There are too many barriers that already exist between God and the not-yet Christian. The church must make certain we are not one of those barriers. Too often, we become the major barrier to bringing God's love to a lost and dying world, particularly when it comes to those who are not like us. Let us pray, "God, help us to become more like Jesus in Philippians 2."

Now that we have a little context, let's continue. I arrived at the restaurant after praying all morning and all the previous evening. I had not yet had the opportunity to discuss personal faith with either Jun or Kira. As I prayed, I sensed God saying, "This will be the perfect time to do that." I prayed that somehow, by the grace of God, these two could come to faith that day.

As we ate, the time came for me to ask the question. You know the question—the commitment question.

We understand the commitment question well in a relationship between two people in love. I dated my wife four years before I felt it was time to ask "the Question." After four years of dating, I asked her if she would consider committing her life to a relationship with me. Had I put that question off, I might still be dating her now, more than forty years later—or I might've lost her to someone else who was willing to ask her!

Now was the time for me to ask Kira and Jun the question. I felt the Spirit clearly nudging me. No doubt, it was risky.

I asked, "Have you two considered becoming Christians?" I was shocked at the response I got.

Kira said, "Pastor, I did that the other day, when I returned home from Bible study. When can I learn more and become baptized?"

I was totally surprised. I thought, *This is supposed to be more difficult!* People are not *really* supposed to be interested in Jesus. I have heard the naysayers remind me many times that people in our day are not interested in faith. "We are in a post-Christian America. These sorts of approaches don't work anymore."

As those negative thoughts poured out of my head and heart, I listened to Kira, amazed that God had done the work. We celebrated the new heart and life she had received from the Master.

Then it was Jun's turn. "Pastor, I committed my life to Christ after church this last week."

I was amazed again. It was supposed to be more difficult than that! Although I have watched this happen many times in my life as a Christian, it always amazes me.

To summarize what happened, the *people of God* (i.e., the people of our small church plant), along with the *Word of God* (i.e., the thirty-minute Bible studies we had shared together) had been strategically brought together with the *not-yet people of God* by the *Spirit of God*—and the miracle of redemption happened! Just like that!

This may seem too simplistic or unrealistic to some, but it has been my consistent experience of now more than forty years of observation as a Christian. Disciple making is the simple result of the people of God engaging with the not-yet people of God with the proclamation of the Word of God. The confluence of these three creates the perfect environment for the miracle of reconciliation to take place.

If you remember my personal salvation story, a person of God (the young man at the beach) approached me (a not-yet person of

God) and shared the Word of God (Matthew 7:13). Finally he asked me, "Will you be one of the few who makes it to heaven?" Boom! In less than an hour, I accepted Jesus and began walking with him for the rest of my life.

I don't want this to sound too prescriptive or mechanical. It would be wrong to assume that individuals, their stories, and their life circumstances will magically change if we simply plan to put these three items together. We must treat every human as a person of value and worth, regardless of their profession of faith or lack thereof. Please don't assume that the simple framework presented here is the perfect recipe for someone to come to Christ. I am only positing that, when the confluence of these three happens, it provides the most fertile environment for redemption to take place. It is clear in Scripture, and in my experiences, that these three key elements coming together produces a kind of divine synergy that often leads to the miraculous redemption of a soul for the kingdom of God. Scripture is loaded with examples!

When Jonah (a person of God) went to Nineveh (the not-yet people of God), he shared the living word God had given him, and reconciliation happened. The Ninevites believed God. They repented and gave up their evil ways and their violence (see Jonah 3).

Jesus and the Samaritan woman at the well illustrate the same principle at work (see John 4).

The parable of the sower and the seed illustrates that the seed is the Word of God (see Matthew 13).

In Acts 2, a person of God (Peter) preached the Word of God to the not-yet Christians (Peter's fellow Jews and all who lived in Jerusalem), which led to redemption and reconciliation with God for thousands of people.

In Acts 3 and 4, we see the same scenario. The people of God engaged with the not-yet people of God, proclaiming the Word of God, and adding thousands to the church.

I submit for consideration a series of diagrams to illustrate this simple truth. We could take lots of time and spend lots of words to describe what happens when one of these components is missing. I will only give brief summaries of possible outcomes.

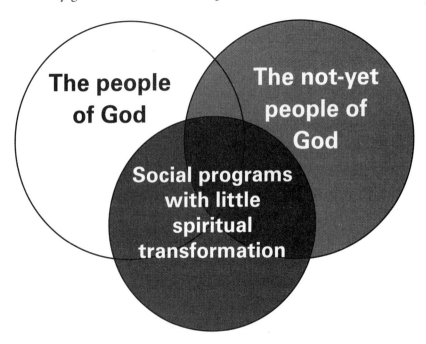

When the people of God approach the not-yet people of God *without* the proclamation of the Word of God, the result is often short-term acts of social justice, immediate physical assistance, and catharsis for those who feel good about doing something to help others. These are good things. No—these are great things. However, this outcome is not the Great Commission. The Great Commission commissions us to make disciples.

There has been a not-so-subtle shift in church culture at the expense of the proclamation of the good news. We say, "Let's simply be present in the world, abound in acts of compassion, bless our communities with justice, and do good things as often as possible without the burden or responsibility of proclaiming Jesus." The shift is clear when some suggest that proclaiming Christ is tantamount to a transactional (or colonizing) action, as if the mere act of proclamation is shameful. Scripture teaches that proclamation and presence (proximity) are essential to make the gospel effective and to make disciples. This presence and proclamation synergy is modeled throughout the Gospels and the New Testament clearly.

There are lots of good, well-meaning churches and lots of well-intentioned Christians doing good things—helping the disadvantaged and disenfranchised, bringing relief to those in bondage and captivity. Matthew 24 tells us we must do these things. We should be about these things naturally as an expression of our living faith in Jesus. However, why would we stop short of sharing the Word of God, which offers abundant life even in the midst of difficult circumstances?

I have learned from my many years of ministry that people who need Jesus expect his people to talk about him. It would be the equivalent of going to a supermarket to find there was no food, or a tire store unwilling to provide tires. The Word of God is *essential* to the work of redemption. Acts 8:1b and 4 remind us that the fledgling church in the first century was made up of people of the Word: "On that day a great persecution broke out against the church in Jerusalem, and all except the apostles were scattered throughout Judea and Samaria. . . . Those who had been scattered preached the word wherever they went." Paul also says as much in Romans 10:14: "How, then, can they call on the one they have not believed in? And how can they believe in the one of whom they have not heard? And how can they hear without someone preaching to them?"

We must beware that we do not become ashamed of the gospel that brings salvation to all who believe in it (see Romans 1:16).

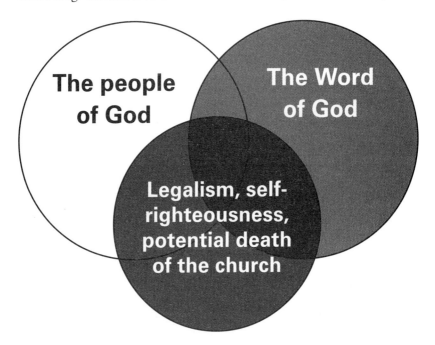

The people of God and the Word of God existing without the not-yet people of God can lead to self-righteousness, legalism, and a siloed people who are isolated from the world to whom God has sent them. In this scenario, the church only grows through birthrate, and can lead to those born and raised in the church environment leaving for more holistic ministries upon adulthood.

For God's church to maintain a missional, theological, social, and biblical balance, there must be a consistent confluence of the people of God, the not-yet people of God, and the Word of God.

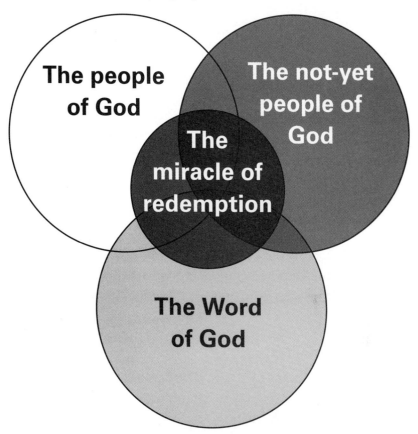

Questions for New Disciple Makers

1. Is your church seeing pre-Christians come to faith regularly?

2. If you were to do an assessment of the balance of your life and the activity of your church, which component would you say is lacking most?

3. What are some actions you could practice to help your personal Christian life and the life of your church find a better balance that could lead to more effectively fulfilling the Great Commission?

SIX

THE DIFFERENT STYLES
OF DISCIPLE MAKING

Many churches today engage in little to no disciple-making activity. Those who are engaged primarily use attractional-only approaches. If we want to reach the lost and dying people whom God loves so much, we need to become more imaginative.

As a minister for more than 40 years, I have discovered the essential importance of Paul's admission in 1 Corinthians 9:22b: "I have become all things to all people so that by all possible means I might save some." When Paul says "all possible means," I think he means *all* possible means! We should be willing to do just about anything, short of sinning, to win the lost to Jesus.

In recent decades, the attractional method has been the primary way churches have engaged in evangelism, outreach, and discipleship. An attractional method looks like programming and activities at the church building that are designed to attract pre-Christians to come and experience church. The idea is that, if we get them in the building, we can convince them to stay and to keep coming back by our hospitality, our preaching, our Christian education, and whatever other programs a church may have going on that would interest someone in Jesus. Once they make a profession of faith, the church works to disciple and equip the new believer in the disciplines of faith so that they become a productive member of the church. The attractional method has satisfied our church-growth appetites but is mostly effective, as Alan Hirsch says, for rearranging the building blocks of the kingdom (i.e., attracting former Christians or Christians from other congregations) rather than *building* the kingdom.

Although we could list several different disciple-making methods from the history of the church, this chapter will focus on the six that are the most familiar and the most practiced. It is important to note that the best methods and practices of effective disciple making have probably not yet been used. The warning is: "beware of old yeast." That is, avoid the temptation of exclusively doing what others have been doing or even what has worked for you in the past. Continue to practice what works, but always evaluate the effectiveness of your disciple-making activities. God is a creative God who knows best how to reach your community with the gospel. He will assist in guiding you to effective methods of reaching pre-Christians in your circles of influence. Give him permission to guide you into new and more productive methods of transforming your community.

Begin with intense prayer times and a focus on the question, "Father, how can we best bring your good news to our community?" God has ideas for reaching the community that no one has yet thought of. Allow time for the Spirit to speak to you and to other people of God regarding how to reach your community. Take the time to listen carefully as he gives you new and creative ways to make disciples in your community.

This chapter is designed to stimulate creative thinking about how to best engage with pre-Christians. The hope is that it will spark a new desire to reach the lost and broken in your community, and drive you to your knees with a broken heart as you listen to God for guidance and clarity on how best to make disciples.

We need to become more like an octopus than an eel in our approach to reaching pre-Christians. Every church should have many tentacles reaching into the community that touch all kinds of people, in all kinds of places, with all kinds of methods. This is how we become all things to all people so that by all possible means we might win some!

Jesus was systematic and strategic in his approach to his ministry on the earth:

1. He proclaimed the coming of the kingdom everywhere he went.
2. He intentionally engaged in the lives of those not yet enjoying a relationship with him.
3. He called perfect strangers to join him in his mission.
4. He lived with his disciples and modeled the behavior that he wanted them to reproduce.
5. He prepared them to be strong in their faith.
6. He released them into service after only three years of disciple-making engagement.

It was a pretty good system. Get among pre-believers and engage them in conversation and relationship. Then give them the Word of God and challenge them to follow him, prepare them for service, and release them to serve.

We may not recognize it, but most of us are also strategic and systematic about the things that really matter to us. Consider this example of our natural capacity to be strategic:

Most everyone reading this book has some sort of income.

Most everyone also has access to some sort of transportation, whether public or private.

Most everyone has a local supermarket.

Most everyone has a refrigerator.

Most everyone has a stove or range.

Most everyone has pots and pans to use to cook food.

Most of us have a table to eat on with serving dishes, utensils, and plates to assist as we consume the food we have purchased and cooked.

Our eating systems tend to work pretty well. What happens when something in this system breaks down? We look to fix it immediately. If we lose our job, we get busy looking for a new job. If our refrigerator or stove breaks, we call someone to fix it, or we get a new one. Why? Because if we don't eat, we die! Our very lives are dependent on us developing an eating system that works.

The difference between a broken eating system and a broken disciple-making system is that, if our disciple-making system fails, others suffer the consequences instead of ourselves. We generally don't feel the consequences of a failing disciple-making system. Those in our community do.

We have difficulty transitioning the idea of strategy and systems for the sacred work of the mission of Christ through his church. There is a tendency to fly by the seat of our pants, haphazardly attempting to fulfill the mission without strategy or planning. If God is strategic in reaching his world, should we not have the same approach?

The goal of this chapter is to provide some tools, ideas, and resources to assist you in developing an effective disciple-making system in your church and life that actually fulfills the Great Commission.

Our tendency in the church is to allow the urgent to crowd out the essential. We concern ourselves first with the urgent issues of paying the bills, keeping our landscaping looking nice, catering to existing members, and working to increase attendance without necessarily focusing on depth of engagement. While we attend to the urgent, the essential task of fulfilling the Great Commission by making disciples gets relegated to the back burner. We will examine six styles of evangelism to assist you in developing a strategic and effective disciple-making system so that the essential gets accomplished. The six styles are conveniently grouped into three broader categories:

1. **Individual disciple-making methods:**
   A. Friendship evangelism
   B. Personal evangelism
2. **Corporate disciple-making methods:**
   C. Church evangelism
   D. Mass evangelism
   E. Compassionate evangelism
3. **Reproducing cells that make disciples**
   F. Church-planting evangelism

No list will cover *every* method used to make disciples. This list is an attempt to summarize the various styles that have worked and been used in the past as well as the present.

In order to have an effective and fruitful disciple-making system, all six styles should be practiced in the life of the corporate church, regardless of church model, so that by all means you might win some! The church and the Christian should be engaging in as many methods as possible to fulfill the Great Commission.

Some will feel more comfortable with one style over others. If you feel you can't see any of these six styles working for you, make it a matter of intense prayer. Ask God to help you find a way to fulfill your commission. Perhaps God will help you imagine something brand new, or perhaps God might help you become more comfortable with one of these six methods. The method, style, or approach isn't the important issue. The important issue is, are pre-Christians coming to faith through your life and influence? If not, find a way to make that happen! God is highly motivated to help you with this. It is not his will that any perish but that all will come to repentance (2 Peter 3:9).

Individual Disciple-Making Methods

A. Friendship Evangelism

Friendship evangelism is the act of befriending someone, building a relationship with them, and earning trust and rapport with them. The hope is that they will see your Christian life, be attracted to the Jesus you serve and, eventually, ask you to help them become a Christian. I like friendship evangelism because I like forming relationships and getting deep in those relationships. I like lifelong friendships and am blessed to have many.

But one of the potential problems with friendship evangelism is sincerity on the part of the disciple maker. I heard a Christian say the other day, "If I present the gospel to someone and they reject it, why would I want to continue to waste my time with them? We have nothing in common now. I need to move on to find those interested in embracing Jesus." It is hard to imagine words like this coming out of the mouth of a Christian, but I heard them with my own ears. Gratefully, after a brief conversation, my brother in Christ began to see that maintaining relationships is still important even if people reject the gospel.

The key to friendship evangelism is sincerity. Find someone who doesn't know Jesus and start a conversation, develop a friendship, and get involved in their lives. It is important to be authentically interested and express that interest so they know that you care about them. Finally, an important component of friendship evangelism is being ready at any time to ask or answer the golden question when led to do so by the Spirit. Every believer can and should be involved in friendship evangelism.

Let me illustrate. Mollie was the mother of one of our college students at church. She was not involved with the church at all. Her religious background and current practice was Buddhism. My college and careers pastor was deeply concerned about her. He thought we could reach the entire family through Mollie. Mollie owned a Thai restaurant, so I went to eat there. On my first visit, Mollie was so happy that her daughter's pastor had come to try her restaurant. A relationship started. I planned to visit the restaurant weekly, and my goal was to visit around one thirty, when the lunch rush was winding down and there might be more opportunity to chat with Mollie.

It worked. The third time I visited, Mollie sat down to chat. I remember her telling me how hard things were in the business. She was having difficulty managing the challenges of life and business. She had been seeing a therapist with little relief. Visits, late lunches, and conversations continued through the fall of that year, and our friendship grew. There were many days when I just sat and listened to her challenges and promised to pray for her. Most of our conversations were not about faith. However, I did pray for her and invite her to church, which she accepted.

Mollie attended church a few times but not regularly. I made it a habit to pray daily that she would soon make a decision to serve Jesus and that God would help her find relief from the difficult challenges in her life. Toward the end of October, she mentioned she had never experienced a traditional American Thanksgiving dinner and asked if our church staff could help her. We set a date to go to Mollie's house and provide her with an authentic Thanksgiving feast.

It was a great time. We cooked turkey and all the trimmings. Once the table was cleaned and everyone had wandered out of the dining area, I sensed a nudge from the Spirit to stay for a while, hoping Mollie would also stay and chat. She did, and we began to talk about the tradition of gratitude at the Thanksgiving holiday. I shared that I was thankful for the way God had saved my life some twenty years ago. I shared how he had helped me find peace and joy in an otherwise unfruitful life with little hope for a happy future.

As I talked, the Spirit nudged me again. *"Mark, ask her if she has considered becoming a Christian."* It was as clear as a bell. It was time to ask the question. I took the risk and asked.

Mollie said, "I thought you would never ask. I've been interested in Christianity ever since my daughter started attending your church. I've been questioning my religion. I don't like the Buddhist answers to eternity. I love the idea of eternity with Jesus and his people. Please tell me how to become a Christian."

I shared the ABCs with Mollie of how to come to Christ.

A: **Admit** you need God and confess your sins.

B: **Believe** in Jesus as your Lord and Savior.

C: **Commit** your life to serving him, and you will be saved.

We prayed together, and Mollie prayed a prayer of forgiveness and acceptance. It was amazing. She quickly became a very serious Christian. It wasn't long before she had to move back to the West Coast to restart her IT career because the Thai restaurant didn't survive. I received a call from her in the spring of the following year. She was coming to see her daughter graduate from college and wanted to be baptized in our church by her first pastor. We had a great celebration and watched her grow in her faith. Mollie became a Bible study leader in her church on the West Coast and continues to serve Jesus today.

Friendship evangelism is effective when we remember the three key components. Let's analyze how these key components worked for Mollie.

I. Find someone who doesn't know Jesus.

The best way to accomplish this step is to pray for God to guide you in your day. Listen and be hypersensitive to the leading of the Spirit as you live your life. One of the great challenges many Christians face is that they have few encounters with pre-Christians. Many believers have so filled their lives with Christian activity and Christian friends that there is little or no time or opportunity for real contact with non-believers. There are probably people in your circles of influence whom you encounter weekly who do not know Jesus. Take the initiative to get to know them.

II. Be authentically interested and express that interest in their lives.

You can develop a deeper relationship with a new friend by showing an interest in things they have interest in. Get involved in activities they enjoy. Dave and John Ferguson have provided an easy-to-remember system using the word BLESS as an acronym to become involved in the lives of others.

B: **Begin** with prayer. My prayers for Mollie prepared her heart and my thoughts and words as we began a relationship.

L: **Listen** to them and show interest in their story. I listened weekly to Mollie's challenges and struggles and offered her prayer support to get through them.

E: **Eat** with them. Many meals and conversations at Mollie's restaurant eventually led to an invitation to her home for a big meal.

S: **Serve**. We served Mollie a great Thanksgiving meal that led to an opportunity to share my faith story with her.

S: **Story**. I had the chance to share my faith story at the Thanksgiving table.

III. Be ready to ask or answer the golden question.

I was ready when the Spirit nudged me at Thanksgiving with Mollie to ask her the golden question ("Have you ever thought about becoming a Christian?"), and the rest is history.

This story can be your story. The importance of listening to and having a hyper awareness of the leading of the Spirit is key throughout the entire process. Obedience at critical moments is essential.

As you think about engaging in friendship evangelism, your biggest challenge may be finding someone who doesn't know Jesus. Ask God to help you make some habit changes so you will have opportunity to engage with and initiate a relationship with pre-Christians. As you pray this prayer, you will be amazed at the opportunities God will show you.

One potential issue to be aware of with friendship evangelism is that we make more personal friends than disciples of Jesus. Although many of the people we befriend may never become Christians, we must be intentional about praying for, engaging with, and inviting people to activities related to Jesus and his kingdom.

When following up with a new friend in friendship evangelism, make sure you find a way to reconnect soon and often. Do you know where to find the person after the initial encounter? Get in the habit of carrying a card with your information on it. This way, if they authentically make a decision, they can easily reconnect with you for prayer, friendship, and support.

You can be a friendship evangelist!

B. Personal Evangelism

Personal evangelism is simply going out to find someone who needs Jesus and starting a conversation with the plan of presenting the gospel immediately and asking the faith question in that first encounter.

This style of evangelism is not for the faint of heart. Most Christians are not comfortable engaging in this form of disciple making because it seems so aggressive. Oddly enough, this is the primary style used by Jesus and most of the New Testament evangelists. Some of these biblical encounters have already been mentioned. Others include:

Nicodemus

This was a brief encounter in John 3. The entire conversation between Jesus and Nicodemus lasts only a few short minutes. Jesus shares the gospel with him, and the conversation ends as abruptly as it began. We are not certain of the final outcome or whether Nick decided to follow Jesus, but we do know Nick was the one who initiated the conversation.

Samaritan Woman

In John 4 we find another brief encounter. Obviously, Jesus went to Samaria for the purpose of meeting this woman, implied by John telling us, "Jesus had to go through Samaria" (v. 4). There was a divine imperative for Jesus to go there and speak with this person. At the well, Jesus found a person needing faith, initiated a conversation with her, and brought her to faith in a short period of time. The conversation was brief but ended in a revival for the woman's town. Not a bad small beginning.

Invalid at the Pool of Bethesda

John 5 tells us this story. Jesus met a man who needed faith and initiated a conversation with him. The man was admonished to go and sin no more, and the conversation ended as abruptly as it started.

Matthew the Tax Collector

In Matthew 9, Jesus encounters a tax collector. He engages him and immediately asks Matthew to follow him, and he does. This is a brief encounter where the golden question comes quite early in the conversation.

Zacchaeus

In Luke 19 Jesus initiates a conversation with a stranger, Zack, which leads to faith.

We could add to the list: the woman caught in adultery, the Gadarene demoniac, Philip and the Ethiopian eunuch, Lydia, and more. The evidence is clear. This form of evangelism was used prolifically by Jesus and the New Testament Christians.

What distinguishes friendship evangelism from personal evangelism is the speed at which the gospel is presented. In personal evangelism, the gospel is generally presented very early in the relationship. In friendship evangelism, the gospel is often presented later in the relationship, after rapport and a foundation of trust have been established.

One obvious potential issue with personal evangelism is neglecting the making of a disciple. Personal evangelism can happen very quickly, and if the evangelist exits stage left without following up to ensure the new disciple has a way to connect with a faith community and become a disciple maker themselves, their faith may not be sustained. The most important aspect of personal evangelism must be the effort to stay in the life of the person. The Great Commission is to make *disciples*, not just converts.

I am a Christian today because of a personal evangelism encounter that lasted only three minutes. You can be a personal evangelist, but it is not for the faint of heart.

Corporate Disciple-Making Methods

Here are a few suggestions from someone who has conducted hundreds of corporate events:

- Please don't be discouraged from sharing a story of the gospel, a short drama about the gospel, a brief message of the gospel, or an exciting story of transformation at these events.
- Remember to keep things light (five to fifteen minutes). A presentation of any kind can be effective.
- Plan pre-registration if at all possible.
- In your promotion for any event, notify prospective attenders that there will be a brief presentation, story, drama, or whatever is applicable at the event.

- Operate with integrity, and be honest with your visitors. You are a church. People who come to a church event expect to hear about Jesus. Don't disappoint them.

- Don't be discouraged if someone thinks you are pushing the envelope just because you share even a brief gospel presentation. Expect there to be some pushback. Remember, Jesus did everything right, and they crucified him anyway, along with many of his followers and apostles later on.

- Get contact information for as many visitors as possible. You must be prayerful and thoughtful to develop creative ways to ensure you get contact information for every visitor present, if possible—but again, proceed with integrity and honesty.

C. Church Evangelism

Church evangelism involves inviting guests to come and see the church family, function, facilities, and faith you love and live. Advantages of church evangelism include the opportunity to as much as double your weekly attendance by exposing your church to the community and the community to your church, thereby reaching many in the immediate physical vicinity of your faith community.

Even if you have a nontraditional location or meeting space (like a house church, organic church, missional community, or others), use the place where you meet most often if space allows. If you simply don't have a physical space, remember that the early church didn't have buildings specifically dedicated to doing church, so they held large events in public settings. The idea of church evangelism is to expose the community to your church *body*, not necessarily to a church *building*.

Church evangelism offers your local church an opportunity to share the gospel with those who attend while also giving the members and regular attenders in your faith community an opportunity to partner together in something significant, creating unity in the body of your church. When the people of the body of Christ band together for something great, a unity results that is difficult to replicate in any other activity. One of the best strategic, missional leaders I know, Dr. Dale Shaeffer, puts it so simply and accurately when he says, "Sweat is the juice of unity!" Beyond unifying the church body, seeing new people in the physical church space builds morale among congregants, which is key for member retention.

One very important possible outcome of a church evangelism event is that it gives your people an opportunity to engage with pre-Christians in a safe environment. Some of the people in your church will not yet be comfortable initiating a conversation with a stranger as Jesus, Philip, Paul, and other New Testament characters did. Eventually they may, but church evangelism is the perfect environment to get them in the practice of engaging strangers and could help individual church members begin relationships with pre-Christians that lead to friendship evangelism opportunities. In order to foster this type of environment, it is helpful to encourage church people to avoid huddling in their insider fellowship circles. If they don't feel comfortable stepping outside those circles, at least encourage them to invite strangers into those spaces and be intentional about including new people in group conversations.

For introverted, timid, or fearful laity, one tool you could implement is to put together a small notecard with three or four engagement questions they can use to start a conversation with newcomers and visitors. These conversations can help establish an initial relationship that could ultimately lead to faith. A few sample conversation starters include:

1. Thanks for coming! How long have you been living in/connected to this community?
2. What made you decide to visit us?
3. Tell me a little about your family.
4. How can I pray for you?

You can develop questions that fit your particular context. The goal is to help your people attending the event to discover some commonality with a visitor that could lead to further contact and a relationship moving forward.

One issue with church evangelism is the tendency of church people to think it is the only style of evangelism to engage in, risking their desire to stop being a "go and get" church in favor of exclusively being a "come and see" church.

D. Mass Evangelism

Mass evangelism is designed to be an event that meets a need or responds to expressed community interest. A mass evangelism event should provide a taste of the gospel to the masses. Although there are some similarities to church evangelism, mass evangelism is typically a much larger scale. Often an event like this would be held in a place other than the facility where you meet for regular worship events and activities, like a local park, a community center, a concert venue, or a theater.

A well-executed mass evangelism event will tell your community, "We are here to serve you." It gives the community the chance to see the church in action. Be prayerful, creative, innovative, and thoughtful about planning such an event. Do it well! A mass evangelism event done well will put your church on the map for community members who might not otherwise know you exist. It provides awareness of your presence and your church's priority to make a difference.

One potential issue with mass evangelism is your faith community becoming an event-driven church. When this happens, everything points to major events, diminishing the importance of the necessary functions of disciple making, community building, and other functions required for a healthy church expression.

E. Compassionate Evangelism

Compassionate evangelism meets the needs of the marginalized, disadvantaged, and disenfranchised in your community with the hope of engaging in relationship, learning stories, sharing stories, and seeking to provide holistic ministry for them. By "holistic," I mean bringing them to faith in Jesus while at the same time working to meet their other life needs. The difference between *compassion* and compassionate *evangelism* is the belief that the *end* goal of meeting a need is not the full belly, the stranger welcomed, the prisoner looked after, or the sick person healed. Instead of being ends, these outcomes are the *beginnings* of holistic ministry in compassionate evangelism. The completion of the work of compassionate evangelism and holistic ministry is to share the gospel in hopes that people become connected to the Father, who can and will (in partnership with the church) provide all needs for the rest of eternity.

Preaching the good news to the poor has been a goal of the people of God from Isaiah to Jesus:

> The Spirit of the Sovereign LORD is on me, because the LORD has anointed me to proclaim good news to the poor. He has sent me to bind up the brokenhearted, to proclaim freedom for the captives and release from darkness for the prisoners.
> (Isaiah 61:1)

So he replied to the messengers, "Go back and report to John what you have seen and heard: The blind receive sight, the lame walk, those who have leprosy are cleansed, the deaf hear, the dead are raised, and the good news is proclaimed to the poor." (Luke 7:22)

Compassionate evangelism is not simply meeting the physical, psychological, and other needs of the underserved and unserved. It is also offering access to abundant life—an intimate relationship with the divine. Providing the gospel gives more than just a filling meal or paying a bill. These are great places to start, but they aren't where we stop. It is not an either-or proposition but a both-and proposition.

I see two extreme positions in churches across North America. On one hand, there are Christian compassionate-ministry centers that focus exclusively on meeting physical, emotional, medical, and other needs while excluding spiritual needs. This position is almost resistant to the gospel as proclamation. In what amounts to a reverse bait-and-switch philosophy, their thinking is that talking about God, Jesus, or the church is somehow disrespectful. Although these ministry leaders understand that developing a relationship with God is the ultimate key to abundant life, they somehow don't want to tell others about it. I have been told by many such leaders that so many people in their care have had such bad experiences with the organized church that to speak about it would be more harmful than helpful. One leader stated that he tells volunteers that talking about God, Jesus, or the church in his compassionate ministry is strictly forbidden. If someone asks a question, they can answer it, but they cannot initiate such conversations.

On the other hand, there are also Christian compassionate-ministry centers that demand the gospel be presented in every venue where compassion is expressed. If a meal is provided, the gospel must be presented in some form verbally. If there is a distribution of items to the community, the gospel must be presented verbally in some format. Many leaders in these ministries will not accept a donation that puts stipulations or regulations upon people who receive the benefit of their donation. These ministries are willing to reduce the number of people they can help in order to avoid having any limitations on a verbal presentation of the gospel. A sort of spiritual pride is at work in these cases. One leader said, "If they think they are going to put a muzzle on the gospel, they can just keep their donations."

The best answer to these two extremes can be found somewhere in the middle. If the mission of the church is to make disciples in the nations, then we should be about making disciples, even in compassionate ministry. Jesus said of his own ministry, "The good news is proclaimed to the poor." So proclamation of the gospel should be included in compassionate evangelism. That proclamation can be performed in a variety of ways. God is so creative and can help us discover ways to get the good news to every person we encounter with compassion. For example, drama is an amazing medium to use to share the story of God. The use of video and other audiovisual tools can make the good news impactful and effective. Compassionate ministries need to be deep in prayer and planning to ensure they are giving their best effort to present Jesus in ways that are positive, helpful, effective, and truthful.

There are two major barriers to effectively doing compassionate evangelism. The first is that there is a sort of spiritual entropy that happens when we do long-term ministry of any kind. The second law of thermodynamics says that entropy always increases with time. Compassionate ministries are most susceptible to this temptation because we develop systems and expect them to continue without regular evaluation and updating.

It takes much prayer, thought, planning, and strategy to ensure that the proclamation of the good news to the poor is both done well and received well. The danger is that humans—even Christian humans—can become complacent over time and simply stop finding ways to be creative and energetic about proclaiming the gospel.

The second barrier is the pressure from various leaders, both worldly and Christian, to provide only resources in compassionate ministry, not evangelism or proclamation of the gospel. I have experienced these pressures, as has any Christian who engages in compassionate evangelism. One such experience I will never forget.

We were in the southwestern part of the U.S., in a city desperately in need of Jesus and resources for abundant life. We partnered with a food bank that was unaffiliated with any church. We had been using their food to provide meals, groceries, and sustenance to thousands of people every month for many years. We provided a weekly meal to the hungry. It was simple. We purchased food from the food bank by the pound. We served the meal, prayed a blessing for the food, and then enjoyed the meal. Afterward, we set up a long table anyone could visit to find fresh vegetables and breads to take home for their families.

This process worked fine for years, but we eventually learned that one participant was offended and complained to the food bank that we prayed a blessing for the meals. As a result, an emissary from the food bank visited to observe the meal. When it came time to pray for the meal, the food bank representative interrupted and said, "You can't pray for this food. It is provided by the food bank, and we don't allow prayer when our food is distributed."

The person who had been interrupted said, "We are a Christian church, and we always give thanks to God and ask God to bless the food we eat." Then he proceeded to thank God for the food and ask God to bless it.

The next day we received a letter from the food bank stating that we could no longer purchase food from their organization, which started a barrage of newspaper articles along the lines of: "Local Church Cut Off from Food Bank because of Prayer." Radio stations called to interview church staff, and city officials called to ask what happened. It was a real nightmare for everyone involved.

We didn't know what to do, so we began to pray intensely for God's help to find food to continue providing for the needs of that community. It was a scary week, but we received an answer at the end of it. The largest wholesale food distributor in the state called. The owner had read the article in the newspaper and offered to begin providing food for our ministries. Praise God, we received so much food that we became a distributor to other churches and ministries who wanted to help the needy. It was amazing to see how God met our need when we decided to include him in the process of our compassion.

I know of ministries that extend compassion to thousands regularly, yet those thousands have no grasp of the good news that can change their lives for the better. After Jesus went through all the towns and villages meeting the needs of the people, Matthew says, "When he saw the crowds, he had compassion on them, because they were harassed and helpless, like sheep without a shepherd" (9:36).

God, guide us from mere compassion to compassionate evangelism. Help us know the best way to present the good news of your gospel to those who need to hear it. Help us to speak the truth in love as we serve the underserved and unserved in our communities. Help us to be courageous enough to guide them to the Shepherd.

The good news is that anyone can do compassionate evangelism! It can be planned as an event and implemented by a church congregation, or it can be personally finding those in need in your community and engaging with them as an individual. Matthew 25:31–46 reminds us that how we care for the least of these is a reflection of our love for God:

> When the Son of Man comes in his glory, and all the angels with him, he will sit on his glorious throne. All the nations will be gathered before him, and he will separate the people one from another as a shepherd separates the sheep from the goats. He will put the sheep on his right and the goats on his left.

> Then the King will say to those on his right, "Come, you who are blessed by my Father; take your inheritance, the kingdom prepared for you since the creation of the world. For I was hungry and you gave me something to eat, I was thirsty and you gave me something to drink, I was a stranger and you invited me in, I needed clothes and you clothed me, I was sick and you looked after me, I was in prison and you came to visit me."

> Then the righteous will answer him, "Lord, when did we see you hungry and feed you, or thirsty and give you something to drink? When did we see you a stranger and invite you in, or needing clothes and clothe you? When did we see you sick or in prison and go to visit you?"

> The King will reply, "Truly I tell you, whatever you did for one of the least of these brothers and sisters of mine, you did for me."

Then he will say to those on his left, "Depart from me, you who are cursed, into the eternal fire prepared for the devil and his angels. For I was hungry and you gave me nothing to eat, I was thirsty and you gave me nothing to drink, I was a stranger and you did not invite me in, I needed clothes and you did not clothe me, I was sick and in prison and you did not look after me."

They also will answer, "Lord, when did we see you hungry or thirsty or a stranger or needing clothes or sick or in prison, and did not help you?"

He will reply, "Truly I tell you, whatever you did not do for one of the least of these, you did not do for me."

Then they will go away to eternal punishment, but the righteous to eternal life.

Compassionate evangelism is for every believer. Find someone who is the "least of these" (however you define it), and begin a friendship and help them. Pray that God will guide you as you seek to connect them to the Shepherd. Remember that what you have done for the least of these, you have done for Jesus.

One potential issue with compassionate evangelism is doing compassion to the exclusion of evangelism that leads to disciple making. Being engaged in compassion means we must always be mindful of and strategic in addressing the Great Commission. Our commission is to make disciples, not only to meet physical and other nonspiritual needs.

Corporate Disciple-Making Follow-Up Tips

One suggestion for those wanting to engage in corporate evangelism effectively is to develop and print a card for every attender from your church in preparation for encounters with visitors. Many regular Christians who are willing to serve at a mass evangelism or church evangelism or compassionate evangelism event are not accustomed to starting conversations with strangers. A pre-printed card will give the more timid and reserved people a tool to help them engage. On the card, list several introductory questions that serve to reduce the stress of starting a conversation with a stranger. Give your people ideas to start conversations that might lead to friendships beyond the event. Obviously, you must think carefully about what questions will work in your particular context, but a few questions that might serve as a jumping-off point for you include:

- How long have you lived in this city?
- Tell me about your family.
- Where else have you lived?
- What sports teams do you follow?
- What special interests or hobbies do you have?

It's a good idea to have a pre-registration link and QR code for your corporate evangelism event, if possible, on all promotional materials and ads. If you have a pre-registration option, you will have contact information before the event even happens, which makes following up so much easier.

Prepare and print connection cards (visitor information cards) for the next regular gathering of your church body.

Assign someone to take pictures or video of the event. Be ready to show a short presentation of the event to the body at your next corporate church event. Showing involvement and engagement will help get more of your people involved with follow-up, even if they were not able to attend the event.

Spread the filled-out visitor information cards across the front row of chairs or on the altar prior to the next worship service. Include a thank you card, an envelope, and a stamp for each family represented by the cards. During corporate prayer, invite your people to come forward and pray for a family represented by cards. After they have prayed, encourage them to take a connection card and contact supplies home with them so they can write and mail a personalized note thanking the visitors for attending the event and inviting them to return for a regular gathering.

Reproducing Cells That Make Disciples

F. Church-Planting Evangelism

Church-planting evangelism should be clearly understood. If we focus on church planting alone, we will start groups that may become mission outposts and possibly (but not guaranteed) some version of the church in the future. However, if we focus on the Great Commission, we will have to plant churches in order to accomplish the mission. Church planting is like disciple making on steroids. A good disciple maker can often learn to become an effective church planter.

Church-planting movements happen when the people of God are centered, focused, and committed to making disciples of the nations. This mission cannot be fulfilled without planting lots of churches in lots of places for lots of people of various backgrounds, ages, cultures, races, and other demographic details.

New churches grow more by reaching new Christians, while more established churches tend to grow by transferring members from other churches. It is time the North American church woke up to the reality that planting churches is not optional. It is essential for accomplishing the Great Commission. It is safe to say, since church planting is the most effective method of making disciples, that God must have a special interest in this method. He wants the entire world to be saved (2 Peter 3:9), and in order to get that mission done, we must use the most effective methods. The most effective method is planting churches.

One potential issue with church-planting evangelism is that we focus on sending Christians off to start a work without the understanding that the goal is to find pre-Christians and bring them to faith. We all know churches that were planted with thirty Christians from other churches that are still exclusively those same thirty Christians twenty years later. Church plants may start as offshoots of existing churches (or they may not), but they root into the soil and culture of the place where they are planted in order to grow and thrive. A thriving church is best defined by the number of pre-Christians who come to faith and are discipled into maturity there. A church is not thriving if new believers are not coming to Christ and being discipled, regardless of size, scope, activities, ministries, gifting of its leaders, or whatever else. A thriving church is one that fulfills the Great Commission.

Questions for New Disciple Makers

1. Does your church have an effective disciple-making system?

2. Do you have a strategy for reaching the pre-Christians in your community? Is it working?

3. Are pre-Christians coming to Christ through your life and through the ministry of your church regularly?

4. Which of the six main styles of evangelism covered in this chapter has the most appeal to you? Why?

5. What activity could you engage in to start connecting to pre-Christians in an effort toward disciple making?

6. Have you ever felt a nudge from the Spirit to consider planting a church or church expression?

SEVEN

FROM DISCIPLE TO DISCIPLE MAKER

This chapter is the foundational reason for writing this book. It is what the previous chapters have all been leading to, namely: *Can a Christian in the church who has never personally made a disciple change to become a disciple maker?*

I have asked around fifty thousand pastors and ministry leaders over the last ten years about their disciple making, and under 5 percent admit to being personally involved with disciple making of any kind. This chapter is written for the 95 percent of church members who have never personally brought someone to Christ. I praise God for those who are actively involved in disciple making! My prayer and hope are that this book will encourage you and others to join in the mission to make disciples of the nations!

This book is for the Christian who is faithfully serving God, attending church gatherings, and supporting the church with their resources. This Christian is willing to serve occasionally in places requested of them and is looking forward to being with Jesus for eternity but has never personally led someone to Christ. According to research, this group is the largest group of people in the church today. It is pretty clear that many Christians in North America have not been personally engaged in making disciples. I believe that can change. The question is *how*, and that is what we want to unpack in this chapter.

Paradigm Shift

How does a Christian who knows they should be making disciples begin the journey to actually becoming a disciple maker? Most of us don't think much about making disciples until we:

A) Read a scripture in our daily devotions that causes us angst regarding our lack of activity in the lives of pre-Christians. Time and space dulls that angst as we go back to our lives.

B) Hear a sermon, listen to a blog, or read an article that reminds us of the Great Commission, creating a brief but fleeting impulse to consider how we could possibly get more involved with disciple making. The impulse passes as we are bombarded with other needs and passions we read or hear about.

C) Encounter a lost and broken person desperately in need of Jesus, causing a sense of grief that passes the further we get from that experience.

Is there a way to keep these impulses and emotions alive so they actually lead us to change our habits and behaviors? Is it possible that we who are reading this now can begin to actually feel the lostness of other human beings, causing us to change our actual schedules and activities to lead us to personally making disciples?

I say absolutely! Let's dig a little deeper into how to move from our seats to the streets to gain opportunities to encounter lost and broken people.

Beth provides my favorite story of a paradigm shift that followed a change in belief. Beth was one of the most vibrant believers I have ever encountered. She was almost born in church. She loved Jesus and loved seeing people come to Jesus. She supported disciple-making efforts with prayer, giving, and enthusiasm. She was a model Christian by most every measure. As her pastor, I preached a sermon called "True Signs of a Mature Christian" in which I mentioned my top four biblical signs of a mature Christian: love, humility, holiness, and disciple making. The strong emphasis of the message that day was that most people leave out disciple making from their mature Christian definitions. Yet how can a Christian be mature and not pursue the one thing Jesus commissioned believers to do, which was to make disciples? We can make disciples and do all the other things as well. God is that powerful—if we are that obedient.

Beth approached me after the message that day with a troubled look on her face. She said, "I am seventy-two years old and have been in the church my entire seventy-two years. I have prayed that God would help me be a mature Christian all along the way. Your sermon today struck me. God has helped me develop the first three things. The last one, I have not. The Spirit spoke to me in your sermon this morning and put me under deep conviction. I can't be sure I have ever personally led someone to Christ. I have been involved in bus ministry. I have been calling on others many Saturday mornings. I have assisted in getting many people to church, but I am confident I have never personally led anyone to Christ." She then referenced the parable of the steward and said, "When I stand before Jesus, I want to have some real fruit. I have not been a good steward of the talents God has given to me in the area of disciple making."

For a moment, the story of Jesus and the rich man who wanted to know how to get into heaven crossed my mind. This was her rich man moment. Should I say something to encourage her? If so, *what* should I say to one of the most godly Christians I have ever had the privilege of serving alongside?

Before I could decide how to answer her, she said, "I want to lead someone to Jesus before I die. Can you help me?"

Responses like that to a sermon make a person think they are speaking to an authentic, humble Christian. Many stories could be recounted of Christians who had a different response to similar sermons, but this time I had encountered a Christian who realized that disciple making is a true sign of maturity in Christianity. She didn't criticize the message. She didn't resist the divine impulse to fulfill the Great Commission. She didn't try to make excuses. She didn't defend her infertility in the kingdom. She took the hit. It was amazing.

I was so flabbergasted at her integrity that I was about to start bragging on her and celebrating her response to God's conviction, but the Spirit stopped me and directed me simply to answer her question, "Can you help me lead someone to Jesus?"

After pausing and recovering from the shock of encountering such a fervent desire to please God, I said, "Absolutely! You can make a disciple. Jesus commissioned you to do it, the Holy Spirit empowers you to do it, and now your heart is broken for it."

Beth and I began an amazing journey together that day, the result of which was a new young family coming to Christ and serving God from that time forward. Beth had a paradigm shift from thinking disciple making was the corporate church's responsibility to accepting it as a personal mission for herself as a member of the body of Christ. Her comments reminded me that the Great Commission wasn't given to an organization, corporation, or institution but to individuals. She had taken the Great Commission personally for the first time in her seventy-two years of Christian experience. For the first time in her faith walk, she believed she was individually commissioned to make disciples, regardless of whether the church organization made disciples. She knew she had to. For the first time, she believed it was a personal commission. Now she was ready to learn how.

Belief is the first challenge to overcome. The thing that curses the modern Christian with inactivity in disciple making is the belief that someone else is ultimately responsible. This curse has been building for many years. The church-growth movement made its contributions by teaching us that the church is the only place where people come to Christ. We were taught to invite people to church so the pastor could give a message that would inspire them to want to change. The worship team would provide music that would make it easy for them to make the decision. The trained counselors or gifted evangelists at church would help them come to faith. Then small groups would provide a place and the relationships necessary for new Christians to grow. Regular worship would keep them inspired, and they would be okay. The "regular" Christian's job was just to get them in the doors of the church. The problem with the church-growth method is that we stopped being personally responsible for making disciples and delegated it to the institution. Laity pay the tithes to fund buildings, programs, and support the professional ministers. This can make us feel good about the growth of the church. Many believers today think this is the best way to advance the kingdom and fulfill the Great Commission. As a result, many contemporary North American Christians feel no personal responsibility to personally make disciples. We overcome this problem by intentionally making a paradigm shift on our belief structure.

The Great Commission wasn't given to a corporate organization but to individual believers. In Matthew 9:37, Jesus said the problem is a worker problem, not a field problem. Jesus was telling the disciples that the need in the harvest field isn't for highly trained, professional, college-educated, seminary-trained, licensed, and credentialed leaders. Jesus says the harvest simply needs laborers. Thank God for those professionals! But the kingdom is advanced through individual workers. The need is for people who are willing to go get "dirty" in the lives of others.

When Jesus called Peter and Andrew in Mark 1:16–17, it was a personal call. In Luke 8:39, Jesus told the demoniac to return home and tell them how much God had done for him. In Acts 1:8, the one definitive attribute of a Spirit-filled believer is to be a witness. Disciple making isn't just a commission but the natural outflow of a true relationship with Jesus. The Samaritan woman showed us what the natural outflow of true faith leads to.

The first hurdle to get past in becoming a disciple maker is believing it is your personal responsibility rather than a corporate responsibility. Jesus never told us to build the church. In fact, Jesus told Peter, "I will build my church." We were not commissioned to build a corporate entity. We were commissioned to make disciples.

Of course, this is not an indictment on the organized church. Good systems, solid structures, and organized strategies are all vital as long as they are contributors to the mission of God. Where we get into trouble is when these things become self-perpetuating rather than mission *strategies*. How can we tell? Good question. If pre-Christians are not coming to faith and being discipled to reproduce, there is a problem with those structures. Something must change to restructure the priority. Disciple making must be at the top of the priority list. The mission (i.e., the Great Commission) must be central, or we are no longer the church but a self-perpetuating organization established under false pretense. If disciples are being made, the church grows. If I focus on growing the church, disciples are not necessarily made, and the mission is lost.

In order for someone to change their behavior, they must precede it with a change in belief. If previously unfertile Christians are to become fertile disciple makers, we must be willing to make a significant paradigm shift in our belief system to a personal understanding of disciple making. God has personally called, equipped, and sent you out to make disciples. You can do it. You are commissioned to do it. Believe it. Expect it. Do it!

Personal Determination to Obey the Great Commission

After a belief change and paradigm shift, becoming a disciple maker for the kingdom of God hinges on your personal determination to obey the Great Commission. Let's review the many words of Jesus on this matter:

Therefore go and make disciples of all nations, baptizing them in the name of the Father and of the Son and of the Holy Spirit, and teaching them to obey everything I have commanded you. And surely I am with you always, to the very end of the age. (Matthew 28:19–20)

He said to them, "Go into all the world and preach the gospel to all creation. Whoever believes and is baptized will be saved, but whoever does not believe will be condemned."
(Mark 16:15–16)

He told them, "This is what is written: The Messiah will suffer and rise from the dead on the third day, and repentance for the forgiveness of sins will be preached in his name to all nations, beginning at Jerusalem. You are witnesses of these things."
(Luke 24:46–48)

Again Jesus said, "Peace be with you! As the Father has sent me, I am sending you."
(John 20:21)

But you will receive power when the Holy Spirit comes on you; and you will be my witnesses in Jerusalem, and in all Judea and Samaria, and to the ends of the earth.
(Acts 1:8)

If we were to combine the verbs to summarize these multiple Great Commission statements of Jesus, it would be something like:

1. Go
2. Preach/Teach
3. Make

Understanding the implications of these three verbs will help us move from disciple to disciple maker.

Go

This seems simple, but it isn't simple for someone who has never gone out to make disciples. It is counterintuitive. It is against social norms. It is contrary to many people's personalities. It is unsafe. It is dangerous. It is risky. Yet Hebrews 11:6 says, "And without faith it is impossible to please God." Faith *presumes* risk. It is impossible to please God without some risk.

God calls individuals to *go* into all the world. That is you and me.

Going means leaving things like safety, security, control, reputation, and social standing behind. We don't like this. We are a risk-averse culture, probably even more in the church than anywhere else.

Go where? Into all the world . . . to the ends of the earth.

For Abraham it was *go* to a place God would tell him later—but for sure away from family and home. For Joseph it was *go* from the safety of home and family to hostile Egypt. For Jonah it was *go* to a strange and notorious place and preach to sinful people. For Paul it was *go* preach to people who fear you (the new Christians), then to people who hate you (the Jewish leaders). For Jesus it was *go* be with humanity and be one of them.

God's call to *go* has been given to everyday, regular people from the very beginning, and that commission and calling have not changed. The only way God's will that none perish can possibly be accomplished is if every believer is in on the mission personally. The corporate church is only as powerful as the individual Christians that make it up.

For the Christian disciple sitting in the local church service each week to become a Christian disciple *maker*, the first action step is to go! Go to where pre-Christians are and proclaim the gospel. It is risky, and it is dangerous. It is also rewarding beyond anything imaginable. I am convinced there are Sauls waiting to hear and to become Pauls. There are Ethiopian eunuchs waiting to hear and to take the gospel to new places today if we would simply go to them with the message.

How do we go? To whom do we go? How do we find, engage in relationship with, and establish rapport with pre-Christians in our God-given commission to go and make disciples?

1. Pray for God's leadership.

As we learned earlier, God is still speaking to God's people. The first rule of becoming a good disciple maker is being in the places where God wants us to be. As shared previously, I have developed the habit of praying five basic prayers each morning:

A) Guide my steps today so that I will be in the places you want me to be.

B) Direct me toward the persons you wish me to start a relationship with.

C) Give me the words I should speak.

D) Provide me with the courage to initiate a conversation.

E) Help me have the wisdom to know how to reconnect with them.

2. Obey the Spirit's promptings.

The stories of Ananias's call to go to Paul, Philip's call to go to the Ethiopian eunuch, and Paul's call to go to Macedonia remind us that God *wants* to network us into the lives of pre-Christians, and it can only happen if we are hypersensitive to his leading. The Spirit still prompts believers today. God knows where lost and broken people are, and God knows where you are. One of the best spiritual practices I have ever discovered is pausing in every personal prayer time to listen to what the Spirit may be prompting me to do and where the Spirit may be prompting me to go. I want to be sure to hear it when God occasionally interrupts my routine and schedule to accomplish his purpose in another person's life.

John 4:4 records that Jesus "had to go through Samaria." There, he met a woman who was in desperate need of God. He initiated a conversation with her and helped her deal with her spiritual condition. She then left and was used to transform her entire community. It all began with the divine imperative, "he had to go through Samaria."

As we pray daily, maybe one of the most important things we can do is remember to pause and listen. The Spirit may prompt you to find your Samaritan woman. Maybe there is a Saul in your community who needs the mediation of the Holy Spirit to be healed of blindness. Rarely does it occur to us that we could be used to assist the next apostle Paul, or the next Billy Graham, to change our world. There is only one way to know who the Spirit wants us to have a conversation with: listen, and allow the Spirit to give us divine imperatives to go to specific places to speak to specific people in order to help advance the kingdom.

3. Begin with those you already know who do not know Jesus.

Recall Beth's story, shared earlier in this chapter. Like Beth, many Christians assume that their associations with family members, coworkers, and friends have already been set. We think it would be too awkward to have spiritual conversations with those we encounter daily when we haven't ever done it with those people before.

I recall having the conversation with Beth about whom she should begin to share her faith with. She told me, "There is a young lady I have been working in the same office with for years. She knows I am a believer, and I am sure she is not. We never broach the subject of Christianity because it is awkward. It could risk both our jobs." I encouraged her to pray and ask the Lord if she should broach the subject with her coworker. When she and I chatted after a week of prayer, she was certain God did want her to have the discussion of faith with her coworker. My response was that, if God was leading her, he would continue to guide and protect her. Well, she didn't lose her job, and her young friend and her family came to faith and are serving Jesus faithfully today. I wonder what would have happened to this young family had Beth allowed the fear of being awkward or of losing her job to win the day. Beware of over-thinking these relationships rather than over-praying for these relationships.

One of the contributing factors to my conversion was the influence of my little brother's faith. I watched him, admired his resolve and commitment to God, and noticed his humble, godly walk with Jesus. I had little interest in God at that time, but watching his life piqued my interest and helped soften my heart for the Spirit to reach me at the beach that day in 1976. Beware of undervaluing your Cristian influence on those who are already in your life.

4. Allow the Spirit to lead you to places where pre-Christians gather.

One of the most challenging issues for Christians is the reality that so many of us spend the better part of our time in the presence of those who already know Jesus. I have struggled with this a great deal. In working for the church, I find it difficult to engage with people outside the church. If I am not careful, every moment of my existence will be spent around church people, at church, doing church activities. I call it Church Vortex Syndrome. It is difficult to make new disciples when one rarely engages with pre-Christians.

God helped me begin to overcome this challenge by directing me to change some of my daily routines and behaviors. Some years ago, when I first recognized my tendency to spend all my time and energy around believers, I began to pray, "God help me to make time to engage with people who do not yet know you as Savior and Lord."

God's answer to that prayer was amazing: a little inconvenient, and sometimes uncomfortable, but almost always fruitful and enjoyable. God clearly led me to change habits and routines, and to begin to go to places where pre-Christians gathered. He helped me overcome the ingrown habits that Church Vortex Syndrome had developed.

I am convinced God wants to do the same for each of us, if we learn to listen to the tender leadings of the Spirit. There are a few specific changes the Lord directed me to make to avoid this trap. I hope that my sharing them can assist you in moving from the vortex of exclusive Christian engagement into communities that are desperate for your presence and influence.

Purposeful Prayer Driving and Walking

The Spirit began to direct me to begin prayer driving and prayer walking in areas of town I had a broken heart for. I committed to one hour a week prayer driving and walking in those places. After a while, I was led to have conversations with people in those places. Soon, I developed a deep compassion for them. Matthew 9:36 says, "When he saw the crowds, he had compassion on them, because they were harassed and helpless, like sheep without a shepherd." The next thing I knew, I found myself offering assistance to and developing relationships with people I would have never encountered in the circles I had been limited to. Eventually, pre-Christians became new Christians and learned to engage in the life of the church.

Strategic Locations

As I prayed for guidance on where to engage pre-Christians, the Spirit directed me to make a few sacrificial changes. I felt led to begin frequenting public Laundromats, which was a challenge for me. I had become so accustomed to the quiet and convenience of private laundry rooms. I travel some three to four weeks a month and usually stay in hotels or Airbnbs. Those places have amazing private or semi-private places to do laundry. I sensed the Spirit leading me to ditch the private places and only use public Laundromats when traveling. Let me confess, this was not a calling to convenience. One thing had become obvious to me: I can only remember a few times in eight years of traveling when I had an encounter with another human being in those private and semi-private places. From the time I began this practice, my encounters with pre-Christians have multiplied.

One of those stories was Tabatha, who managed one of the public Laundromats I ventured into one Mother's Day Sunday. Many of my fears and preconceived notions about these encounters were challenged that day. The Spirit impressed me to go to the Laundromat that morning to distribute flyers for a Mother's Day celebration planned for that evening at our new church. My intent was to pay the laundry costs for every mother in the place. As I dropped quarters into the machines, it was easy to share about our event later that evening. I went through the entire Laundromat, paying for laundry costs and handing out flyers to every mother in the place.

As I was about to leave, I noticed the manager watching me. I began to think, *I better get out of here. She might ban me from coming in and talking to people. She probably thinks my presence is bothering her customers.* I found myself stealthily sneaking out to avoid an encounter with her that might jeopardize my future opportunities to engage with customers there. I made it past the last aisle of dryers and out the door. I turned toward my car, feeling triumphant to have made an uneventful escape.

Just before I could get into my car, here she came, almost running. "Sir, sir!" she shouted.

I was busted. I stopped and prepared myself for the lecture about bothering the customers.

She said, "Can I come to your Mother's Day event this evening?"

Boy, had I misjudged that encounter. I proceeded to give her a flyer. She and a few other mothers from that morning attended the service that evening. Tabatha even accepted Christ that night.

Later, after several months of hard work and proof of sobriety, she was able to regain custody of her children. She began attending church, found a husband, and is living an amazing life today. She often reminded me that that day at the Laundromat was the turning point in her life.

Wow, who knew? God knows where to place us. He knows where to place you. He knows whom you and I need to encounter to share faith with. The key is to listen as he seeks to direct you to those strategic locations. Go to those places in faith—not in fear, expecting the worst, as I did that day—and go, believing that you have a divine appointment.

Intentional Courageous Conversations

The Spirit also impressed me to make conversation with servers at restaurants a priority, and to take seriously whatever they told me was happening in their lives. This turned out to be one of the most amazing disciple-making practices I ever engaged.

After a few contacts with McDonald's drive-thru personnel, I would ask for prayer needs. It was amazing! We saw numerous new believers and their families come to faith and begin attending church within a few months of these encounters. In one church plant, we saw twelve to fifteen new faces regularly as a result of a conversation with one McDonald's manager. Most of these transformation stories began with a Christian showing genuine interest in the employee—stopping by regularly, assisting with needs and concerns in the employee's life and family.

The courageous conversations were usually as simple as, "Is there something I could pray about for you and your family?"

One such conversation led to the opening of a floodgate of family challenges, financial concerns, and eventually spiritual conversations that led to life change and deliverance from alcohol addiction. Ultimately, that woman became the matriarchal foundation of a new church plant and of her family moving forward.

I have heard it said that the problem with most Christians is that they have Arctic River Syndrome—frozen at the mouth. Allow the Spirit to give you the insight to have courageous conversations. You may be the only Jesus people will encounter. You have more influence than you might think. You represent the Master to the pre-Christians in your life. The apostle Paul said, "Since, then, we know what it is to fear the Lord, we try to persuade others" (2 Corinthians 5:11).

Preach/Teach

The Greek word for "preach" literally means "to speak forth." It is related to the Greek verb *kērússo*, which means "to cry or proclaim as a herald." This meaning really shows us that we should be announcing, heralding, or proclaiming. This is what happened when the Holy Spirit came at Pentecost in Acts 2. People were given the gift to speak forth as they had never spoken forth before. Stephen spoke the Word boldly in Acts 7, and the result was that Saul became Paul. Stephen had probably never preached a sermon before that day. He did okay!

It is reported in Acts 4:31 that they "spoke the word of God boldly" after they received the Spirit. After Stephen's stoning, we are told that "all except the apostles were scattered throughout Judea and Samaria" (8:1). Then we are told that "those who had been scattered preached the word wherever they went" (8:4). This means the laity—not the apostles, not the super Christians, not the well-trained and experienced and particularly gifted, but *laity*—preached the Word!

It is important to acknowledge that the advancement of the kingdom of God in the early stages of the church and beyond was primarily done by laity—what we today would call "average Christians." This is the best news ever! We don't have to be particularly gifted, skilled, trained, or experienced in order for God to do great things through us. Two primary examples in Acts are Philip and Stephen. The great work of Paul in bringing the gospel to the known world was really catalyzed by a layperson's sermon. Simply put, God entrusted the gospel to laity. He trusted the laity to spread the gospel through proclamation in the first-century church. He still trusts laity to do the same today!

Proclaim!

Make

"Make" is an interesting word Jesus uses. Jesus says that the making of disciples is *our* work. He doesn't say, "Go, and *I* will make the disciple." He puts that responsibility on us. He tells his disciples to go and *make* disciples. It is obvious to any studious Bible reader that only God can change a heart, so how do we reconcile Jesus commissioning us to make disciples when we all know only God can transform a heart? The command makes perfect sense if we understand God's provision. It would be impossible for any believer to make a disciple without the four gifts God gives to enable disciple making: 1) his son, Jesus; 2) his Word; 3) his Spirit; 4) his prevenient grace.

God's Son, Jesus

Jesus is both an example for us and a companion to us. A relationship with him encourages us on our journey. Jesus assures us that he is with us always, even to the end of the age. The best disciple-making training I can imagine is to read the four Gospels and learn how Jesus made disciples. Jesus was the best disciple maker ever, and his escapades are recorded for us to learn.

I encourage you to read the Gospels and take notes. Ask questions: Where did Jesus meet people who needed God? How did he encounter them? How did he initiate conversations with them? How soon did he ask the golden question? How did he make disciples out of them? How long did it take for Jesus to make a disciple?

Once we figure out the answers to those questions, the simplest way for us to make disciples is to imitate what Jesus did.

God's Word

Hebrews 4:12–14 gives us a picture of the power of the Word of God. The Word of God is alive and active. A little word study tells us that the word for "alive" is the Greek word *zoe*. The word for "active" is *energós*. His *energy* can be described as living energy for us to take on our journey into disciple making.

I can testify to the power of God's Word myself. When I was five years old, a pastor said to me, "Mark, the Bible says, 'Behold I stand at the door and knock. If anyone hears my voice and opens the door, I will come in and share life with them.'" When I turned seventeen, that word she planted in my heart when I was a little boy found sunlight and nourishment. Today, that seed has completely taken over my life. Every living moment, it controls my life. The Word of God is living energy! Use it when you share your faith. Plant it into the hearts of pre-Christians and watch how the Spirit grows it. Nothing of value in the kingdom will happen without the proclamation of his Word.

God's Spirit

God's Spirit is given to guide us, empower us, and protect us. It has power to make us larger than the sum of our parts. The Spirit gives us the spirit of Jesus. In John 14:12, Jesus reminds us that we can do the things he did. Even greater things can we do than he did because he is back with the Father and the Spirit has been released. The Spirit gives us the power to leave things we would not normally leave, to go places we would not normally go, to speak things we would not normally speak, and to believe things we would not normally believe.

In Acts 1:8, Jesus tells us we receive power when the Spirit comes on us. We need to be reminded that the power we receive from the Spirit is:

mountain-moving power;

sea-parting power;

lion's mouth-shutting power;

furnace-cooling power;

wall-busting power;

sermon-reaching power;

world-reaching power.

This is the power you and I receive when we receive the Spirit. Does this sound like an "average Christian's" power? No! This is power to transform disciples to disciple makers!

Christians are not to be defined by our weakness and incapacity to go, to speak, to believe, and to see the miraculous. The coming of the Spirit at Pentecost changed all of that. According to Paul, those weaknesses have been made perfect because of the Spirit (see 2 Corinthians 12:9). If you are afraid, God's power is made perfect in that weakness. If you are timid, God's power is made perfect in that weakness. If you are weak, God's power is made perfect in that weakness.

If you are a Christian, you are not average, and you have this same power that has been on display in the lives of "regular" people throughout history! You have the power to go be witnesses everywhere. Let His power flow through you as he has through "average" people in the past. The Spirit turns everything right side up for the person of God.

God's Prevenient Grace

Prevenient grace is grace that goes before us. God has given grace to go before us to prepare the hearts of those who need Jesus for an encounter with us. John 4:38 tells us, "I sent you to reap what you have not worked for. Others have done the hard work, and you have reaped the benefits of their labor." The Spirit has done the hard work. We are called to go and bring in the harvest.

In 1976, God prepared my heart before that young man ever spoke to me at the beach. I had experienced four tragic, premature deaths in the two years prior to my encounter with the young man. I lost my best friend, Toni, who died by gun violence at age sixteen while attempting to purchase drugs. Another friend, Jimmy, died at age eighteen while tripping on LSD. My brother Allen was killed at age nineteen in an auto accident after partying at a bar. And my brother-in-law Larry was killed at age twenty in the same auto accident as Allen.

When I met the young man at Virginia Beach at age seventeen, I knew those four deaths were the result of nefarious activity. I was so ripe for someone to talk to me about changing my life that it was palatable. I thought about dying all day, and about eternity every night prior to that encounter at the beach. God used these horrible tragedies to extend his prevenient grace to draw me, to prepare me and my heart for that day that resulted in my transformed life.

The good news is that every person on the planet who doesn't serve God is, at this moment, being drawn by God's prevenient grace through circumstances in their lives. We know this because the Scripture tells us it is not his will that any perish (2 Peter 3:9) and that no one comes to Jesus unless God's Spirit draws them (John 6:44). At this very moment, God's Spirit is at work in the life of every person in your neighborhood or sphere of influence who doesn't have a saving relationship with Jesus. They are being drawn and prepared by his prevenient grace for an encounter with a Christian like you! That is great news! He has done the hard work already, and he calls us to go gather up the harvest. If God has done all of that, the least we can do is respond by gathering them into the kingdom.

I wonder how many people God has ripened, yet no one is there to harvest? Let's be ready and eager to go fill our buckets!

In Conclusion

Jesus made disciples by meeting pre-Christians. He engaged in conversations with them. He walked with them (human to human, day in and day out, in their daily activities). He asked them the golden question. And he taught them to obey everything he did.

Jesus is our best example.

Make disciples!

Moving from being a disciple to a disciple maker is simple but not necessarily easy. It's just four steps, but they take time and intention:

1. Pray for and allow the Spirit to change the paradigm in your mind from thinking the corporate church is singularly responsible for the Great Commission. Embrace the truth that the Great Commission is the ultimate responsibility of every believer. The Great Commission was given to individual Jesus followers, not an organization or institution.

2. Determine to personally obey the Great Commission by going to places where pre-Christians gather and forming new relationships. Be bold as you go, and be prepared to proclaim the good news to them as you show authentic interest in who they are, in who their families are, and in what is going on in their lives.

3. Invest in relationships that lead to making disciples for Christ.

4. Repeat!

Questions for New Disciple Makers

1. Do you believe God could use you as effectively as he used Stephen or Philip in Acts?

2. If no, why not?

3. If you were to take the Great Commission personally and seriously this week, where could you go in your community to encounter and engage with pre-Christians?

4. Will you pray daily for the Spirit to lead you into relationships with pre-Christians that can result in a new disciple being made?

5. It has been said that the longest journey in the entire world begins with a single step. What are the first and second steps you will take to become a more effective Great Commission disciple of Jesus?